The Little Book of Big Questions

How did the universe begin?

Can machines think?

What is life?

by Jackie French

illustrations by Martha Newbigging

Annick Press Ltd. • Toronto • New York • Vancouver

© 2000 Annick Press Ltd. (North American edition)
© 2000 Martha Newbigging (illustrations)
© 1998 Jackie French (text)
Original edition first published in 1998 by Allen & Unwin Pty Ltd., Australia
Designed by Sheryl Shapiro

We acknowledge the support of the Canada Council for the Arts, the Ontario Arts
Council, and the Government of Canada through the Book Publishing Industry
Development Program (BPIDP) for our publishing activities.

Cataloging in Publication Data

French, Jackie
        The little book of big questions

ISBN 1-55037-655-1 (bound) ISBN 1-55037-654-3 (pbk.)

1. Questions and answers – Juvenile literature. I. Newbigging, Martha. II. Title.

AG195.F73 2000 j031.02   C00-930584-X

The art in this book was hand drawn, scanned and then colored in Photoshop.
The text was typeset in Charlotte and Burweed.

Distributed in Canada by:
Firefly Books Ltd.
3680 Victoria Park Avenue
Willowdale, ON
M2H 3K1

Published in the U.S.A. by Annick Press (U.S.) Ltd.
Distributed in the U.S.A. by:
Firefly Books (U.S.) Inc.
P.O. Box 1338
Ellicott Station
Buffalo, NY 14205

Printed and bound in Canada by Kromar Printing Ltd., Winnipeg, Manitoba.

visit us at: **www.annickpress.com**

Contents

To Josh, who keeps asking questions,
and to Edward, who doesn't like my answers!
—J.F.

To Eva and Del. Thanks for putting up that
chalkboard by the kitchen table when I was three.
—M.N.

Why this book?

**Do aliens exist? How did the Universe begin?
What happens when you die?
Why isn't life fair?**
Is there anyone in the world who can answer
these questions, and be sure that they're right?
The trouble is, the bigger the question, the more
possible answers there are.

What killed the dinosaurs? See pages 89–90 for seven possible answers.

What happens when we die?
Well, there are more possible answers for that one than will fit in this book.

**Well, why have you written a book giving us lots of questions and no
clear-cut answers?**
That's a good question. I wrote this book because a bit of an answer is
better than none at all—just as a bit of chocolate cake is better than none.
    But I also hope these answers will inspire you to ask **more** questions, to
find **more** answers—more pieces of the big puzzles that face humanity ...
Remember, there's no such thing as a dumb question!

**Where did we come from? When will the Universe end?
How are we different from animals?**
People who ask "How?" or "Why?" (or "Why not?") are the ones who keep
on inventing new machines, new ways of looking at the world around us.
Asking questions is one of the things that makes us human.

How did the Universe begin?

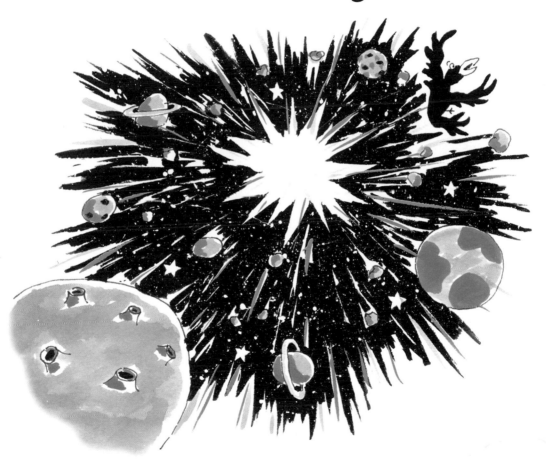

How did the Universe begin?

Good question. Let's go on to another one … Oh, all right, I'll have a go at it—but don't blame me if you get confused. **Everyone** is confused about this one—or they should be. Even Einstein didn't have the answer. Okay—first option …

The Big Bang

This is a nice, dramatic idea—that once the Universe was very small and dense, then suddenly it went "whoooosh." (Actually there wouldn't have been a bang—sound needs to travel through something to make a bang, and before the Big Bang there wasn't anything.) It's still whooshing now; in fact, it seems to be expanding faster than ever.

You mean we're in the middle of a supergalactic explosion?

No. The Big Bang doesn't mean that there was something small that exploded and all the bits are going everywhere—like a potato if you put it in the oven without putting holes in it first (do **not** try this!).

Then how can the Universe expand?
Does that mean we're all getting bigger?

Some of us are getting fatter.

No. What is really happening is that the space between galaxies is stretching. It's just like kids being let out of school. Suddenly the door opens and they run out as fast as they can—and instead of being crammed up in a classroom, they fill the playground. There aren't more kids—and the kids aren't getting any bigger—but the space **between** them is getting bigger, so they cover more area.

But where did the Universe come from in the first place?
From nothing.

How can you make something out of nothing?
Okay, so I can't make a cake from nothing—I need eggs and flour and stuff—and if I tried to make a Universe from nothing, then there'd be nothing in it.

But scientists think we started from a Universe containing **zero energy**. Matter—the stuff things and people are made of—has positive energy. Gravity has energy too—negative energy. Put the negative energy together with the positive energy, and they cancel each other out.

So maybe the Universe exists, but if you add it all up it comes to nothing.

(I did say this was confusing … If you want to know more about the Big Bang, look up the "Where to ask questions" section at the back of the book.)

Lots of Big Bangs

With this theory the Universe is made up of many areas that keep expanding —like a mass of bubbles that all produce new bubbles—and we may never

know about them because we can only see such a tiny fraction of the Universe.

There's another theory …

The Universe has always been here

It's possible the Universe never began,
because it's always been here.

You mean there never was a time when it wasn't?
Yes—and matter keeps on being created at the center of the galaxies, like bubbles producing new bubbles producing new bubbles, all expanding.

There are lots of arguments against this, though. For example, according to the Second Law of Thermodynamics, everything runs down in time. Your flashlight batteries go dead, your glass of Coke loses its fizz, you run out of energy—and so will the Universe. And if the Universe is using up its energy now, then it can't have **had** energy for ever and ever.

The complicated theory

(Don't ask me to give a simple name to this one!)

Another idea is that **time** and **space** have always existed, but **matter** hasn't—it arose due to quantum vacuum fluctuations. Don't ask me to explain this one either—I don't understand quantum vacuum fluctuations at all—but if you look up some of the books listed on page 126, you'll discover more.

All these theories (I think) agree that the Universe is expanding—even if they don't agree on how or why.

How do we know the Universe is expanding?
In the 1920s a scientist called Hubble noticed that very distant galaxies give a redder light than galaxies that are closer to Earth. When something moves away, light waves get "stretched" and give off a redder light—so these far-off galaxies must be hurtling further and further away from us. Hubble worked out how fast the Universe is expanding. Other scientists have worked backwards from that to discover how old the Universe is.

How old is the Universe?
Hubble reckoned that the Universe was
2 billion years old. Nowadays people think it's about 12 billion years.
The Earth is at least 4 to 5 billion years old (we can tell that by measuring "radioactive decay").

How far away are the stars?
Stars are too far away to measure in miles or kilometers,
so astronomers use light years.
A light year is the distance light travels in a year.
One light year is nearly 10 million million km
(or 6 million million miles)—
that's 10 with another 12 zeros behind it!

Our giant galaxy

Our galaxy is called the "Milky Way" because the part of the sky it's in looks "milky" with so many stars. It's the second-largest of all the galaxies in its group (well, we can't be the biggest and best all the time ...) —it's about 130,000 light years across.
The largest galaxy in our "neighborhood" is the Andromeda galaxy.

What was here before the Universe?
Some people say "nothing"—no space and no time either. Time doesn't begin until space does. Sounds odd, doesn't it?

But if I looked at my watch two seconds before the Universe began ... ?
Not possible. Because there was no matter. So no you, no watch, and no time.

What do religions say about how the Universe began?
All sorts of things.
◊ That "God" created the Universe;
◊ that it exists only in the mind of God;
◊ that it was given form by the thought of God;
◊ that it has always existed and so it didn't need to start;
◊ that it has never really existed but we just think it has;
◊ and many others!

Some people believe it's blasphemous even to ask how the Universe might have been created, because that's the same as saying God couldn't have created it.

Do you think that?
No. I think all we're doing is stating **how** it evolved—not Who did it or why.
   I can tell you how a seed grows without denying that God exists; so why can't we study how the Universe grew?

What does the Bible say about how the Universe began?
According to the Book of Genesis,

   In the beginning God created the heaven and the Earth. And the Earth was without form and void; and darkness was upon the face of the deep. And the spirit of God moved upon the face of the waters. And God said, Let there be light; and there was light.

And if you think that sounds a bit like some of the scientific descriptions … well, other people have thought so too.

Does the Bible say anything about how old Earth or the Universe is?
In the 1600s, the Irish Archbishop Usher (who didn't own a calculator, a computer or even an abacus) worked out that the Earth must have begun in the year 4004 BC. He did this by adding up all the references to time in the Bible—especially the "Begats."
   The "Begats" is an enormously long list of who was the father of whom:

13

And Arphax lived five and thirty years and begat Salah.
And Salah lived thirty years and begat Eber.
And Salah lived after he begat Eber four hundred and
three years, and begat sons and daughters.

And so on for a long time!

Will the Universe ever end?
Probably. But don't worry about it.

Why not?!
Because by then you'll be dead, your friends will be
dead, the Earth will be dead, the sun will be dead …

What will happen when the Universe ends?
This is another question that has lots of answers—and
if you ask it again in 100 years' time, the chances are you'll get quite different replies, because we'll have observed a lot more about the Universe.

◊ It could be that the Universe will stop expanding and get smaller and
denser—and more and more unstable. Then there could be another "Big
Bang," with everything starting all over again.
◊ Or maybe the Universe will expand forever—but the stars (among them
our sun) will gradually run out of fuel and go out, and so life will end all
over the Universe.
◊ Or … There are a million maybes, ones we haven't even thought of yet.

Cannibal galaxies!

Our galaxy—and other giant galaxies—exert a huge gravitational force or "pull" on smaller galaxies. When the smaller galaxies get close, they'd be ripped apart by those same gravitational forces, sending suns and clusters of suns hurtling in all directions.

NB: Do not panic—the distances are so vast and the time it takes is so enormous that we don't have to worry about stray galactic debris … probably.

What will life be like in a million years' time?
Different.

Yes, but how different?
Well, there definitely won't be any humans.

Why not?
All species die out eventually—or they change. Half a million years ago our ancestors weren't human. They changed over the eons and through different conditions, and eventually produced us humans. In a million years humans might have died out. Or evolved into some quite different creatures, and we'll have been their ancestors.

So you're my great, great, great, gre

15

What is life?

How do you tell if something is alive?
Well, something that's alive can **reproduce** itself. Two cats can give you kittens; two cars will never give you another car, no matter how nicely you ask them.

But a crystal will grow other crystals, and it isn't alive.
A crystal is really just changing form—not growing.

So is there any other way to tell if something is alive?
Things that are alive **respond**. If you kick me, I'll yell. If you give a plant light and warmth and moisture, it will grow.

So how do you know if something is really thinking or feeling or reacting, or if it's just a robot or computer programmed to look as if it thinks or feels?
That's a good question. I don't know the answer.

When did life begin?
Life on Earth began about 4 billion years ago, but the earliest evidence we've got are fossilized bacteria from about 3.5 billion years ago. (Dinosaurs were around about 135 million years ago.)

Early life forms were able to reproduce them-selves and **evolve** into more complicated life forms—that's another part of being alive. There's more about evolution on pages 37–38.

If you leave left-over pizza out at Night, I will eat it.

So how did it all start in the first place?

There are lots of theories. (Yes, I know I've said that before!)

◊ Maybe a comet or asteroid hit the Earth, bringing the basic elements of life—water, carbon dioxide, methane, nitrogen and hydrogen sulfide—and enough energy as it hit the Earth to transform these into more complex compounds, the ones people call the "building blocks of life."

Scientists have described a possible chemical reaction with positively charged molecules attracting negatively charged ones, and finally one of the molecules evolving till it was able to create its own energy and replicate itself (reproduce itself exactly) … and, bingo, you had life.

◊ Other people argue that molecules containing carbon, oxygen, and hydrogen could have evolved (when they were exposed to radiation or electricity or lightning) into a longer chain that could duplicate itself, until finally these evolved into RNA molecules (ribonucleic acid) and DNA (deoxy-ribonucleic acid). And single-celled organisms evolved into ones with hundreds of cells or millions or billions—into bacteria, algae, fungi, simple plants, animals, and humans.

Source of life on an asteroid?

Two asteroids in our solar system seem to be covered in reddish carbon- and nitrogen-rich materials. They probably fell out of the "Kuiper belt" of comets beyond Pluto. In this belt, they are out of the way of other asteroids that might crash into them, and too far away from the sun for their rich outer layer to evaporate. Asteroids like these might have collided with Earth a long time ago—just possibly, life on Earth may have started from their carbon- and nitrogen-rich compounds.

What does it matter, if it was so long ago?
Well, if all it takes to start life going is just a simple chemical reaction, then we might find living things all over the Universe. But if the beginning of life was an incredible coincidence, then there probably aren't any aliens—not even alien mushrooms or bacteria.

If it's a chemical reaction, will we be able to make life in a test tube one day?
Maybe. A team of scientists at the Scripps Institute in California have found combinations of proteins that can reproduce themselves and do other things that living systems can. They think that they have created very simple life. Even if they haven't, they or other researchers may do so in the future.

What happens when you die?

What happens when you die?

When you die and are buried, your body rots down into the soil. (Even if you're burnt, the atoms that were your body return to Earth somewhere.)

But doesn't some part of you live after your body is dead?

Many people believe that after your body dies, your spirit or your soul survives. But as to what happens after that, opinions differ.

◊ Some say this spirit goes to "heaven" … or rejoins a universal soul.

◊ Some say it becomes part of the spirit of the land around you … or part of things you've loved.

◊ The Inuit, who live in the Canadian Arctic, believe your soul lives forever. When you die, your soul stays for a while in the female spirit's special place, but soon returns to Earth to become another human or, perhaps, an animal such as a wolf, caribou or dog.

◊ Buddhists and others believe that your soul survives and comes back in another body (not necessarily a human body), and it keeps on doing this until "perfected," and then it never has to return to this Earth … The Dalai Lama says, "I think of death as being like changing your clothes when they are worn out, rather than as some final end." The Dalai Lama, like most Buddhists, believes that your state of mind at the time of your death influences the quality of your next rebirth.

◊ Other religions believe that the same thing happens to everyone, no matter how you've behaved.

◊ Hindus believe that what you do in this life affects what will happen in your next life. Your soul will continue to be reborn until it's pure.

◊ And some religions don't particularly care what happens when you die—they are more concerned with how people act while they're alive.

◊ You might not believe in souls at all, but still see people living on in others—either through their unique contribution to their children's DNA (if they have children) or in memories.

I like being alive!

Should you be scared of being dead?
No. Either you won't know or feel anything—or you trust in your God to protect you.

Then why are people scared of dying?
Because if we weren't scared of dying, we wouldn't take care to stay alive. I remember the first time I realized I really would die. (I'd known about death, of course—but realizing that other people die and accepting that **I'll** die one day are very different things.) It made me angry—it just wasn't fair that I should die. I instinctively wanted to stay alive, just as I want to eat and drink and breathe air. I **like** being alive! And then I realized that humans have to want to live, have to want it very keenly, in order to survive.

If we hadn't wanted to live, we'd have just rolled over and said "Hi, little pussy cat, come and have a bite!" when a saber-toothed tiger chased us. And that would have been the end of the human race …

What do you think happens after death?
I don't know. Maybe what happens after death just isn't understandable by people who are still alive. My feeling is that religious descriptions of life after death are trying to put into human terms something that is too utterly different for us to understand. And then of course there may be nothing after death at all.

Is there any evidence of life after death?
Some people who have stopped breathing and then been "brought back to life" have seen a long white tunnel with a feeling of a bright light and incredible goodness at the other end. This is called "a near-death experience." But many other people who have also stopped breathing (i.e. they were clinically dead) and then been revived didn't see anything at all.

But don't the visions that some people have prove there must be something after death?
No. Medical experts say you can get visions like that when your brain doesn't get enough oxygen. But the visions **could** still be a true picture of what happens after death.

What about people who say they can remember their past lives?
I get a bit suspicious about most people's "past lives"—they seem to pick only well-known parts of history to have lived in, like ancient Egypt or Babylon ...

But there have been other children or adults who have had "memories" of things they couldn't have known about in their present lives, so they feel they must have lived before and been "reincarnated" (born again).

And sometimes people who have been hypnotized have been able to "remember" past lives. Some of these "memories" have been investigated and turned out to be about things they'd read or seen when they were small children, and had forgotten … and a lot have just been hoaxes.

Do you think all memories of past lives are hoaxes?
Definitely not. But I don't think that they prove reincarnation either. Sometimes I get a vision of another world that's so clear it's almost as if I'm living in it. So I sit down and write a story about it. I know that these worlds come out of my imagination.

But maybe some people aren't as comfort-able with the idea of imagining another world—perhaps they think the fact that they can see it so clearly means it must be real.

Other people believe that memories can be passed on from one generation to another, without any physical contact—so you might still be able to remember someone's past life without ever having been that person.

Is there any other information about life after death?
Lots—but it's not the sort that you can prove. (The fact you can't prove it doesn't mean it's not true. Lots of true things can't ever be proved. I just

saw a squirrel pass my window; but I can't prove it. I think chocolate is delicious—but I can't prove that either.) Many people just feel a strong, secure faith that their lives—and death—rest in the hands of God, and that everything will be well. Many people will tell you they feel the spirit of a friend or grandparent with them, looking after them.

And other people have faith in Jesus or Buddha or Muhammad or their ancestors' stories, and believe that what they say about life after death is true. Just because you can't prove your belief doesn't mean it isn't true.

Have people always believed that there's a life after death?
I don't know—but the belief does go back an incredibly long way. Graves of Stone Age people have the remains of flowers and beads and weapons in them—as though the people who buried the dead were giving them presents for the life to come.

Not every culture has believed in an afterlife. And in certain cultures it was thought that only some people survived after death. The Ancient Egyptians, for example, believed that royal people had a life after death, because they were descended from the gods; but they thought that ordinary people like you or me who weren't descended from a god just turned into dust.

Does dying hurt?
If you die because you've been badly injured, your injury will hurt … but **being dead** can't hurt because the nerves will no longer be transmitting pain.

What about zombies?
Zombies are dead people who have been charmed back to life. But they're not themselves any more—they just do the will of the person who controls them. They don't rot away like corpses in a grave—but as they pass you get the faintest whiff of death. Nothing can stop a zombie, because they don't feel pain or fear. Even if you chop off their arms, they'll keep on coming.
    (P.S. You only get zombies in books and horror movies—not real life.)

Where did the idea of zombies come from then?
Maybe from hypnotized people—people who'd do whatever they had been hypnotized to do without noticing anything around them. People who have been hypnotized can sometimes put up with an incredible amount of pain—and not realize it till they "wake up."

What about vampires?
Vampires live forever, as long as they can go back to their coffin at night and have fresh blood from a living person—well, that's the accepted story.
    Actually, they aren't true either. We get most of our ideas about vampires from the European legends that Bram Stoker used in *Dracula* 100 years ago. Other cultures have their own horror stories about blood-sucking animals—and if you've heard any about vampire bats, they do exist, even if they hardly ever bite humans.

How long will I live?

Maybe five more seconds. Possibly for 80 or 90 years.

Maybe your life will be **much** longer with new research into artificial organ replacement. Maybe it will be **much** shorter because of pollution, war and/or new diseases.

How can I live longer?

You're just hoping I'll have some magic answer, like eat a certain herb that will let you live to 120.

Eat the right food (i.e., **lots** of fruits and vegetables and not too much fat), get lots of exercise, have enough sleep, spend your time doing fulfilling things, have good friends, be happy, avoid lunatic drivers, too much sunlight, cigarettes, and other dangers ... and the chances are you'll live a long time.

But who knows? Maybe you'll live a super-healthy life and then a meteor will crash down on you tomorrow.

(P.S. It almost certainly won't.)

How long?

Given all the changes in the world, how long do you think you'll live?
How long would you **like** to live? (Methuselah in the
Bible lived 900 years. It's always seemed
a nice age to me ...)

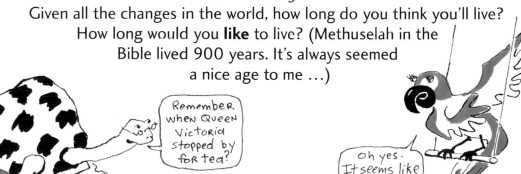

Remember when Queen Victoria stopped by for tea?

Oh yes. It seems like yesterday.

What about having your brain frozen? Doesn't that mean you can live forever and be brought back to life whenever you want?

This is called cryogenics—your brain or your whole body is frozen till science discovers a cure for what killed you or a way to transplant your brain into an artificial body. So far no one has frozen a human brain and brought it back to life again, but the technology is improving all the time and it may be possible in the future.

How about the suspended animation you see in movies?

This is usually based on freezing a whole person and keeping him or her alive for thousands of years while traveling from one galaxy to another. Even if it works one day, it won't keep anyone alive forever.

The great woolly mammoth hunt!

A Japanese scientist hopes to breed woolly mammoths by finding sperm from frozen woolly mammoths and injecting them into cows' ova. Frozen woolly mammoths have been found in the Siberian permafrost. The meat of one was said to be so well preserved that some of it was cooked and eaten— even though it had been dead for 40,000 years. (NB: Do not eat meat that has been in your freezer that long—freezers are not as effective at preserving food as permafrost.)

But even if a mammoth is found, by using ground-penetrating radar, there are many ways the scheme could come unstuck—for example, the sperm might be damaged, or the calves could be infertile (i.e., unable to produce offspring). So it will probably be a long time before you see baby mammoths frolicking in the fields as you drive along.

What about cloning? If I get sick, can't they just clone a new me that'll be just like me—and keep on cloning new me's forever and ever?
To clone a plant you grow another identical plant from a few cells of the first plant. This is very common—many of the plants in nurseries have been cloned.

The first cloned animal was Dolly the sheep. Other animals have been cloned now too—so it's possible to produce clones of the best meat- or milk-producing cows in the world. Or mass-produce cattle that have been genetically engineered to produce drugs in their milk.

Can you clone dinosaurs?
That's very unlikely. Dinosaur DNA would have decomposed by now.

What about *Jurassic Park*?
In the film, dinosaur DNA was supposed to have been taken from an insect trapped in amber (fossilized tree sap). No one has been able to get any DNA from insects trapped in amber—and it's even less likely that you'd be able to get dinosaur DNA from the guts of biting insects. But it was a great idea.

Can you clone humans?
It hasn't been done, but it's probably going to be possible soon. Many

countries are passing laws against cloning humans—but it may still be done illegally somewhere.

What would happen if I were cloned?
You'd have a twin—someone with exactly the same genes. But it wouldn't be you, any more than natural twins are each other. When you clone a human—or an animal—you don't clone their memories. The kind of person you are depends as much on your experiences and memories as on your genes.

So cloning doesn't mean we could have a million Hitlers?
No. You might have lots of twins of Hitler … but they might grow up to be artists (Hitler wanted to be an artist) or kindergarten teachers—a lot would depend on who influenced them as they grew up and taught them what was right and wrong. You'd never get anyone exactly like Hitler because the clone would not absorb the same ideas as he was growing up.

Could we clone people from the past?
Not yet. When a 3,000-year-old human skeleton was dug up near the Cheddar Gorge in England, scientists were able to match its DNA with the DNA of a history teacher who lives within 20 miles of the Gorge; so the history teacher must have been a direct descendant … but the skeleton's DNA probably wouldn't have been complete enough to clone him with the knowledge we have now. In 20 years' time it could be a different story.

Researchers claim to have DNA from a 2,500-year-old Egyptian mummy. Imagine cloning one of the Pharaohs … Would he grow up to be a brain surgeon? Rubbish collector? Math teacher?

Will there be lots of clones of live people in the future?
Possibly. A few people might want to have twins of themselves instead of having a child that has another parent; and people who can't have children might choose to have a clone created.

We might also be able to grow clones so we can use their hearts, kidneys, blood, and so on—but **should** we? This is something we need to start thinking about.

Should we transplant pig hearts or chimpanzee kidneys into humans?

At first I thought "Yuk, no" and then I thought "Hey, wait a minute. If I eat pigs, then why can't I have a pig heart? What's the difference?"
But somehow I still didn't like the idea …
And then I thought, "What if my son would die if he didn't receive a pig's heart?" I knew there was no way I'd see him die if there were any means of saving him.
But what if it meant a risk of breeding new diseases?

What do **you** think?

Spare-parts you
Imagine you had a clone of you—
without a brain so it couldn't think or feel.
How would you feel about using its heart or kidneys?

What do **you** think?

What were the first humans like?

Where did the first humans come from?
Early humans—our ancestors—probably came from Africa, just like our relatives the apes and gorillas.

When was that?
People have found remains of "hominids" (relatives of humans, just as tigers are relatives of the cat next door) that are about 4.5 million years old. These were *Ardipithecus ramidus* (meaning "ground ape" and "root")—they are at the root of the human evolutionary tree. They probably walked on two legs like us, but had ape-size brains.

   About a million years later came *Australopithecus afarensis*: hominids a bit more than a meter (3 feet) high, with short legs and long arms. They would have looked more like apes or gorillas than humans, but they had bigger brains than apes, and walked on two legs and probably used tools— rocks to crack open shellfish and so on.

So what about the first humans?
The first member of the human, or "Homo," family was *Homo habilis* (handy man), who appeared about 2.5 million years ago. Their brains were definitely much larger than those of apes, and they **made** tools instead of using rocks or sticks that were handy.

   Then there was *Homo erectus* (upright man), who looked pretty much like modern humans except that they had such low foreheads and small chins, and finally our group, *Homo sapiens* (wise man).

Which group were the Neanderthals in?

They were *Homo erectus*.

Who were the Neanderthals?

Neanderthals were people who lived tens of thousands of years ago. They are named after the Neander Valley in Germany, where the first remains were found. Neanderthals in movies are muscular, hairy, round-shouldered, and look dumb. They also carry stone clubs and maybe knock a dinosaur or two on the head for breakfast. In fact, dinosaurs died out long before any of our relatives came on the scene.

The round shoulders are wrong too. It happened that the first Neanderthal skeleton that was found was of someone who had bad arthritis— and the skeleton was hunched over just like someone today who has bad arthritis and is in a lot of pain. But later skeletons showed that Neanderthals stood upright, like us.

The bones we have suggest that they probably did have big muscles (and big brains); but as for being shaggy—who knows? They didn't leave any photos behind, and their skins and hair disappeared thousands of years ago.

Did Neanderthals act like humans?

We don't really know. All we have left of Neanderthals are a few skeletons, tools (knives, axes, and scrapers made of stone and bone), and some graves and fireplaces. That's all we've got to go on, to help us work out what they ate, and how they hunted and buried their dead and made tools. They probably talked, but not as well as us—their voice boxes weren't as developed as ours.

They probably looked after sick people, too. One Neanderthal skeleton was damaged as if the person had been in a rock fall long before death; he had a withered arm and leg and may have been partly blind. He could only have survived if he'd been looked after.

Neanderthals buried their dead with flowers, we think—there's pollen in Neanderthal graves.

Are Neanderthals cave people?

Not really. Some of them lived in caves—as did some of our ancestors; but in most places there just weren't enough caves to go around. Most of them probably made shelters from grass and bark and skins and other material.

What are you?

Try combing your hair over your face. If it lands in your eyes, you're a *Homo sapiens*, but if the bone ridges stick out so much that your hair parts neatly on either side of your face, maybe you're a long-lost *Homo erectus* …

What makes us human?

Talking? Writing? Laughing? Drawing and painting?
A sense of right and wrong? Asking questions?
Using tools?

What do **you** think?

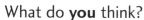

Why does everyone think we once lived in caves then?
A lot of the evidence we have of our long-ago ancestors comes from caves, because that's where you're likely to find drawings and paintings and fire-places from long ago that haven't been destroyed by rain and wind.

Were Neanderthals our ancestors?
Lots of people say no, but there is still some disagreement about this. Scientists worked out that all humans can trace their ancestry back to a single woman who lived in Africa at least 200,000 years ago. They called her "Eve" as a joke. But she wasn't a Neanderthal. It is possible, however, that when our ancestors migrated to Europe they interbred with the Neanderthals.

Were our ancestors black if they came from Africa?
No. They were more likely brownish. Those that stayed in Africa adapted to the sun and became darker, and those that went into cold areas grew paler. It looks as though groups of Eve's descendants walked out of Africa 100,000 years ago and gradually replaced all the human "cousins" all over the world.

Maybe you're part Neanderthal Raccoon.

It could very easily not have happened, though. There's some evidence that our ancestors nearly died out; at one stage there were only about 10,000 humans left. All the billions of people on Earth today are descended from them—so a kid in Boston could be more closely related to a kid in Iceland than two gorillas in the same patch of forest in Africa are to each other. Our ancestors must have been real survivors, able to adapt to the cold, dry, Ice Age conditions that wiped out all our "cousins", like the Neanderthals.

All these theories are regarded as blasphemy by many religious groups. Some Christian sects, for example, believe that the world was created 6,000 years ago, with humans already exactly as they are now. They find it impossible to believe that we share the same ancestors as animals— chimpanzees and other apes. (In the 1800s, many white people in Britain were ready to believe that they were related to chimpanzees but could not accept they might have the same ancestors as black Africans.)

IS evolution just a theory?

No. Evolution itself isn't a theory. You can watch it happen in a laboratory when you breed fruit flies. You can get hundreds of generations of fruit flies in a few weeks —and so you can watch them change or "evolve."

It's a bit like dog breeding—people mate the smallest dogs they can find so they produce smaller puppies, and these small dogs are bred with other smaller dogs, till in the end we have a breed of dog that is quite different from the original parents and is able to sit in someone's pocket instead of wandering the tundra.

But **how** and **why** and **when** things in the past have evolved—and how and why and when humans evolved—well, that's theory.

Why do things evolve?

Good question. (I always say that when I don't know the answer.)
◊ Mutations (changes in genes caused by aging, radiation, etc.)?

◊ Chance?
◊ Changes in the environment so "natural selection" works differently?
◊ Or you might answer "God."

What is "natural selection"?
"Natural selection" works like this. If a green frog moves into a brownish pond, then it's likely to get eaten by a bird. But if one frog is brownish already, its tadpoles are more likely to survive (Nature selects them) and the most brownish of **their** kids will survive too. So after many generations there may only be brown frogs in the pond.

Could we be descended from space aliens?
We might be—but probably aren't. There are too many fossil bits of people who look increasingly like modern humans to think that we didn't evolve here on Earth.

Could space aliens have genetically modified Earth species so that humans evolved ?
Again, they **could** have—but even aliens probably wouldn't have started an experiment that would take 7.5 million years.

How are humans different from animals?

How are humans different from animals?
Of course humans are different from animals.
We use computers. We watch TV. We wear clothes.
But take away our machines and our clothes …?

What if a child were brought up by apes?
Would it act like an ape or a human?
Well, it wouldn't be able to speak English or use a computer—but it wouldn't be exactly like the apes either. It would probably be more adventurous and **much** more enquiring, and make a bigger range of sounds than the apes. And as soon as it met other humans, it would learn at least some human habits quickly—and its ape companions wouldn't.

But what REALLY makes us humans so different?
Well, we can speak.

Can't any other animals talk at all?
Gorillas and chimpanzees can be trained to speak sign language. They can even teach sign language to each other. Various monkeys use at least several different cries, and so do geese.

Your pet dog probably understands many words of our language, like "walk" and "dinner" and "bed" and "car" and "NO!" Chimps and dogs and other animals can comprehend even two or three words put together, like "bad dog," "Go way back!," "Find the ball!" or "Get in the car!"

But they probably can't understand "I put the bone under the mat because it smelt good and I wanted to get it later." And they certainly can't tell the difference between "I put the bone under the mat because it smelt good" and "I think I might put the bone under the mat in case it smells good tomorrow."

And no matter how many words your dog understands, it will never be able to **say** them.

Hey am I human? I can talk. I laugh and I ask questions.

Why can't other animals talk?
For the same reason other animals can't laugh. Raccoons chirr like birds, dogs wag their tails,

No silly, you're a cartoon animal.

river otters chirp, and chimps make panting noises —but even if you think your dog is laughing at you, it doesn't go "Ha ha." If you want to speak—or laugh—you have to be able to control the way you breathe out. Try it—say something and see how you break up your breathing into little bits.

Humans are probably the only animals that can control their muscles well enough to be able to speak. Other animals can make a few sounds—but there's no way they could say, "How now brown cow? I see the sea's blue."

What's so good about being able to talk anyway?
One advantage is that if you can talk, you can communicate in the dark— which is really useful if you want to say, "Watch out, there's a giant poisonous spider on your left shoulder" or even "Once upon a time there was a kid just like you …"

It's also probably easier to develop concepts (abstract ideas) if you use words instead of sign language. It's easy to make up a sign for "water" but probably harder to find one for "truth."

Can you make up a private sign language?

Try making up a private sign language for yourself with a friend.
Pretend that neither of you can talk. Take it in turns to make up signs
for something you can see, like *dog, car, window*.
Easy, isn't it? All you have to do is point to something
so your friend can see what you're on about.
Now try to make up a sign for *truth, trouble, impossible* ...
How easy is it?

(P.S. If you're really interested, you can look through
the dictionaries of sign language at the library.)

**Do people have to be taught to talk? Or do they just do it—
as babies learn to crawl all by themselves?**
People have to be taught a particular language—but we're probably born
with a built-in ability to talk. When scientists studied deaf kids who'd been
taught to lip-read instead of learning sign language, they found the deaf
kids had made up their own sign language to talk to their parents—even
though no one had taught them.

What other things make us different from animals?
◊ Humans use tools—but raccoons can unhook tightly closed garbage-can
tops and open garage doors, and I knew of a dog that taught itself to turn the
heater on when it was cold and the owners were out.

◊ We work together—but lions and wolves work together when they hunt too. And bees have an incredibly complex social organization, and "dance" to communicate with each other.
◊ Humans can make fire. Or can we? (Can you make fire without matches?)
◊ Humans have art. But bower birds in Australia decorate their bowers. And both chimpanzees and an elephant in the San Diego Zoo have been taught to paint.
◊ We have religion.

Do any animals have religion?
Well, who knows if animals have religious ideas or not?

Actually, it seems unlikely, because having moral or religious beliefs means having abstract thought, and that (probably) takes more intelligence than dogs and cats have. (A dog knows what *walk* and *dinner* mean, but it can't understand *love, hate,* or *beauty* because they aren't things it can look at or smell or eat.)

Whales may be capable of abstract thought—their brains look as though they have the same areas that deal with concepts as ours do. But we haven't been able to understand much of their language yet—and mostly they don't appear to understand us!—so it's hard to tell how they think.

Are we really more intelligent than animals?

We've taught bits of human language to animals, but we still don't know any words (or signs) of chimpanzee or whale or dolphin language. (The psychologist Konrad Lorenz did work out some "words" of "Goose" … but I don't think the geese ever understood him when he tried to use them.)

Do you ever get the feeling your dog is jumping around trying to get you to do something and thinking, "Why can't they just **understand**?!!"

What do **you** think?

Why not just ask us?

How can you tell how intelligent an animal is?

Because you can't just **ask** an animal how intelligent it is, we have to judge by its behavior. In any case, animals' abilities are so **different**. I am better at math than a lion (I'm terrible at math), but a lion can work out how fast a gazelle is going and hunt it down much, much better than I can.

The possum is not a very smart animal. It is quite timid and when faced with something unfamiliar will just stand there frozen. When faced with something scary it will faint.

So what can we do better than animals?

◊ We can learn new things much more quickly. Language is a help here, of course—one human can teach another.

◊ We co-operate better. Other species do too—but usually in only a few ways. Humans are always working out new ways to do things together. Every time you and your friends plan a party or do homework together, you've co-operated—and co-operation seems to be one of the main ways that species and individuals survive. Again, language is a great help.

◊ We are probably the most adaptable species, too—we adapt to nearly all climates on Earth.

◊ We are capable of much more abstract thought.

◊ We may be the only species to have a religious or moral code.

◊ Some people claim that the main difference between humans and animals is that humans have souls because we were made in the image of God. Others argue that we are all just manifestations of a universal soul.

What is a human?

A human is a two-legged animal that knows little about climbing trees.

45

So maybe we're just **more** of a lot of things—more intelligent, more capable of abstract thought, more capable of moral decisions, much better at communication … and much, much more adaptable. Humans adapt, and change things, and invent and ask questions. But I mentioned that before.

Do animals really think—or do they just act by instinct?

Some people claim that the main difference between humans and animals is that animals only ever act instinctively. They say that animals don't think about what they do—they just act, like a computer that has been programmed.

The philosopher and the mouse

When the famous seventeenth-century philosopher Descartes cut off a mouse's tail to see if it could feel pain, he decided that the yelp from the mouse was just an instinctive action. He thought that all animals were just "automata"—machines made out of flesh. Descartes thought that only humans were really conscious—and that all animal reactions were just instinctive.

What do **you** think?

Do you agree?
I've lived too long with animals to accept that they don't think. Try watching a cat working out the best way to get into the house, or the best way to attract our attention so that we will feed it.

My cousin's dog was hungry. It doesn't have its own dinner bowl ... so it picked up the cat's bowl and dragged it into the dining room as a signal to those dumb humans, "Hey, I'm hungry too! Feed me!"

I suspect that animals don't think as much as we do, or about such a range of things.

Do humans have instincts too?
Of course. I jump when I hear a loud noise without thinking about it. When women get a sudden scare, they may jump up on something, while men might respond by hiding behind or under something. This is instinct—something born in us that we don't think about.

Can animals recognize themselves in a mirror?
If a bird sees itself in a mirror, it thinks there's another bird there—and either attacks it or chirps in a friendly sort of fashion. A few animals, though, do seem to see themselves—chimps, orangutans, and maybe dolphins. (In one experiment the chimps were put to sleep, then blobs of paint were put on their faces. When they were facing mirrors they saw the paint and cleaned it off.)

Human babies understand what they see in mirrors when they are between twelve and twenty months old.

P.S. Try holding a mirror up to your dog or cat—and see what happens.

Or get someone to hold a dog biscuit up behind the dog so it sees it in the mirror. I bet it will try to grab the biscuit from the mirror, not bend round to get it—unless of course it can smell the biscuit.

Do animals play games?

Foxes will "play bow" to each other, signaling that they want to play fight. Otters will slide down snow slides, and killer whales off New Zealand play Frisbee with stingrays, tossing them up into the air before they eat them. Dogs chase sticks and balls. Cats pounce on wool as you drag it along the floor.

Many scientists say that this is practicing survival skills. Dogs chasing sticks are really practicing chasing their prey; the whales are showing their babies how to get dangerous food into position without being stung. The cats are chasing … well, you get the idea.

But are our games any different?

You could say that soccer is just a form of practice warfare, one team against another—there's a theory it began with people kicking the heads of vanquished opponents. Hockey and ball games are teaching us how to catch our dinner, even if we don't catch it any more. Board games teach us … well, I bet you can work out some practical use for any game. Or is that irrelevant now?— do we play games for fun, and animals too?

What do **you** think?

Can people be invisible?

No. If you're invisible, you don't interact with light—and if you don't interact with light, you can't see. Gravity can bend light, but light near the sun gets bent by less than 1/100th of a degree; so to bend light around a person—well, you'd need something pretty big.

See-through animals!

Truly—well, almost.

Yes, I said no one can be invisible, but some deep-sea squid and a few other sea creatures are almost totally transparent. Transparent animals don't have pigment cells or blood vessels.

(NB: Although the creatures may be transparent, the stuff they eat isn't. Can you imagine the Invisible Man drinking beet soup and swallowing spaghetti? Yuk. Not to mention what the contents of his stomach would look like when everything started to digest ...)

Should we treat animals differently from humans?

Should we treat animals differently from humans?
Yes, animals should be treated differently—just as you'd treat a baby differently from one of your friends. A baby needs looking after and can't make the choices you or I might.

We can make decisions that animals can't—and we'll probably always make decisions for them, just as we would for a baby. But if you mean is there any difference between hurting an animal and hurting a person— well, I think both are wrong.

Does everyone agree that hurting animals is wrong?
No. Some religions and many people believe that animals were put on Earth to be used by people, so we can use them any way we want. Others believe that we should hurt animals as little as possible—but if it's necessary for humans' food or medicine or comfort, then we have a right to hurt them.

Should we ever hurt animals?

Think about it—you might say straight away that we should
never hurt animals in any circumstances.
But what about testing new drugs on animals to save human lives?
(Drugs are tested to see if they produce cancer or harmful side effects.)
Or cutting the tails off sheep to save them from being eaten alive by
maggots? (Maggots breed in the wet, smelly wool on
the tail.) Or killing animals to eat them?

What do **you** think?

Why do some people choose not to eat animals?
There are many reasons why some people don't eat meat.
◊ They may feel that eating meat isn't healthy. (Eating a lot of meat—especially fatty meat—is bad for you.)
◊ They may have religious reasons not to. Some religions say you can't eat some kinds of meat, or meat that has been killed in certain ways. The Old Testament of the Bible, for example, forbids eating pigs, or animals like horses or donkeys that don't have cloven feet—and so the Muslim and Jewish and other religions that follow the Old Testament forbid eating those foods. Some Buddhist sects do allow their priests to eat meat—but only if someone else puts it into their bowl as a gift.

The ancient Greek philosopher Pythagoras didn't let his followers eat any meat because he believed that every soul came back as something else, so you might eat a human's soul. He even believed that beans might have human souls as well. (No, I don't know why.)
◊ Some people don't eat meat because it means that the animals must be hurt. They hate that hens are crammed into tiny cages, and cows and pigs are kept all their lives in barns and hardly able to move, let alone to go out-side to graze; they hate the way that cattle are killed in abattoirs.

But this alone doesn't mean that eating animals is wrong—just that treating them this way is wrong.

Can you produce meat without hurting animals?
Yes—but not a lot of it.

We grow most of our food at my place with wild animals wandering among the fruit trees, and our hens lead happy lives scavenging beetles and scratching up the lavender. (Hens eat meat too—beetles, worms, lizards, small snakes, baby rats. They also eat "waste"—weeds and scraps; our hens think waste peaches and avocados are pretty good.)

This way you can still grow meat to eat without making any wild animals homeless or having them suffer. You can't produce much meat for eating this way—but you can produce some.

It is possible to kill animals without hurting them, too—our hens don't know what's happening when we chop their heads off.

Are there any other reasons for not eating meat?

Yes. It is literally impossible for the Earth to produce enough meat to feed everyone the sort of meaty diet that most people in North America have—there isn't enough room for the animals to graze, and even if they are kept in barns, their food still has to be grown somewhere.

A lot of the meat eaten in the USA and Canada is from animals that are fed on wheat and corn. The world could feed a lot more people if everyone just ate the wheat and corn instead of feeding it to animals.

BLACKBIRD PIE!

Mind you, you can't always do a simple swap. Much land isn't fertile enough—or doesn't get enough rain—to grow crops. To produce the most food possible in areas like this, where the soil is less fertile, it's better to raise animals—and eat them. The question is "Which animals?" A lot of pasture land in Australia, for example, is turning into semi-desert because cattle and sheep feet are too hard and heavy on the soil, and the animals eat the grass down to the roots, leaving nothing there to keep the soil from being washed away. Also, chemicals containing antibiotics are fed to cattle to prevent diseases, and these chemicals stay in their bodies and end up in the meats we eat.

Are there animals that don't hurt the soil?

All hoofed animals hurt the soil to a certain extent. But there are many wild animals that make their homes in the forage that is grown to feed cattle. These include deer, coyotes, reptiles, and ducks. In many parts of the world, small numbers of birds such as barnyard hens and geese are kept without any harm to the environment.

Wild animals are usually well adapted to their environment, so we could eat them. But in most parts of the world there are now so many humans, and so few wild animals, that we might easily wipe them out.

Isn't eating certain animals disgusting?

Why? A lot of food is disgusting when you think about it—yogurt is milk that's going bad, and eggs are baby chickens that haven't been allowed to hatch. Because we're used to them, we don't vomit when we're invited to eat eggs.

Crocodile meat tastes good; crocodiles can be farmed without being cruel, in a way that doesn't hurt the environment … and, after all, a crocodile would eat me if it could. Why shouldn't I eat a crocodile?

Isn't it safer just to eat fruits and vegetables—then we KNOW we're not hurting anyone?
Are you sure? What about the pesticides that kill insects and the birds that eat them? The herbicides that kill frogs?

Generally, cropland displaces some species and benefits others. Growing crops can create mono-cultures, which are not good for wildlife diversity. The rule of thumb in managing pastures is to take half and leave half, and that way you can hope to accommodate all the species, plant and animal.

Are there any other reasons for not eating meat?
Yes, there's one very good reason—but it's a bit harder to understand than the others.

Humans aren't very good at respecting other animals. We cut down their forests and jungles; we make them work for us—often under cruel condi-tions—and we eat them. If you choose not to eat animals, you're telling them, "I think you have as much right to live as I do. I won't exploit you by using you as food or fur or leather."

Do YOU eat meat?
Yes. And I do respect animals, too. I think you can eat animals and respect them.

Hey, how about if we just eat chocolate cake because it doesn't have any feelings at all.

Except that chocolate cake has egg in it and the eggs may have been laid by imprisoned hens and someone may have cut down a rainforest to grow the chocolate and... and... and...

A large part of my life is spent trying to persuade other humans to let animals live in safety, and to make the area where I live a good place for animals to live as well. Animals kill other animals and eat them—but they also respect each other.

I'm an animal too. I'm part of the circle of existence: I kill and eat, and one day I'll die and be eaten too—not by a lion or tiger probably, but by a million micro-organisms that will help me decay into the soil, where trees and other living things will grow from my body.

I like the idea of my body being eaten by other things.

So I eat meat, but I won't willingly cause an animal pain; I do not think I have more right to a piece of the world than a horse or a cow, just because I'm a human; when I grow my food I'll make sure that I'm leaving space for animals and growing more food for them too—and I'll do whatever I can to let animals live in dignity.

But that's just your point of view.
Yes. Many people think the way I do—and many people have different opinions.

56

Then who's right?

You can decide that one. Until a few decades ago most people thought human beings had rights but animals didn't—so we could do anything at all to animals. There'll probably be lots more discussion about this in the future.

What about cannibals?

Humans mostly don't eat each other—unless they're starving and the social rules break down.

In some cultures, though, enemies eat part of each other—like the liver or heart or brain—either to make themselves seem even scarier or maybe to absorb part of their enemies' courage. There have been other places where you ate part of people you had known as a sort of memorial.

Are there any cannibal animals?

Chickens will eat a dead chicken—but that might be because they aren't intelligent enough to know that it's a chicken.

A mother dog will eat a dead puppy—but that might be because leaving it around could attract beasts that would kill and eat her other puppies. Snakes eat other snakes, crocodiles eat baby crocodiles, rats will eat baby rats, and male rabbits can tear up baby rabbits. Fish and several species of shrimp eat their own or their neighbor's offspring. But generally, animals don't eat their own species.

Do animals have feelings?

Of course they do. Animals feel pain and hunger and fear. But they probably aren't feelings just like our feelings. Many animals, like elephants and whales, do seem to mourn their dead. They try to look after sick members of the herd, too.

Some animals, like geese, mate for life—and if the mate dies, they are never really as close to any other goose, even if they do breed with them. Dogs can grieve for days or even months if their owner or playmate dies. And of course all animals can feel pain or be unhappy if they're forced to live in a way that doesn't suit them.

The trouble is that it's sometimes hard for us to understand animals' feelings. People can be cruel to animals even when they mean to be kind, for example by feeding foods to them that they may have trouble digesting. (That's why you see signs at the zoo saying, "Please do not feed the animals.") They really are different from us—and it's often cruel to them to expect them to live and act in human ways.

Do some animals have to be killed?

Okay, your best friend is being attacked by a crocodile.
Do you kill the crocodile to save your friend? (If you answer "no" to this one, you'd better not let your friend hear you.)

Your best friend is being threatened by a disease that's spread by rats. Do you kill all the rats to save your friend or yourself from the risk of disease?

What if the disease were spread by bears? Would you be prepared to risk seeing all the world's bears exterminated too?

What do **you** think?

(NB: If your friend is being attacked by a crocodile, don't take too long to think about it.)

Actually we usually don't have to make these choices. Rats do spread diseases, but we can make our homes and restaurants rat-proof. And if bears spread diseases, we might be able to immunize the bears or protect ourselves in other ways, just as you wear long sleeves to stop mosquitoes biting you.

I believe that sometimes it may be necessary to kill animals—but that we should always look at alternatives first.

I also think that if we killed everything that might possibly threaten us, the world would be a very empty place.

Can machines think?

Can machines think?

This is a question that leads to lots of other questions—the first one being "What do you mean by thinking?" (Another one is "How are machines and people different?")

When you add 45 and 91 together, you have to think about it. But when a machine adds or multiplies, is it really thinking, or is it just reacting automatically to your finger on the button? Is it behaving a bit the way insects do when they operate by instinct? ("Automatically" and "by instinct" are often equated with not-thinking.)

What about a more complicated area of thinking, like making decisions? Can machines make decisions? Do you have to understand time or have a concept of the future before you can make decisions and have ideas?

Maybe self-awareness is part of thinking. Machines are already able to process information faster than humans can—but will they ever be aware that they're doing it?

What does "self-awareness" mean?

Being self-aware involves at least two levels of thinking—you are thinking one thing and noticing yourself thinking about it at more or less the same time. Humans are always thinking and feeling about things that aren't immediately in front of us. A computer does the jobs it's been set to do ... but our minds wander all over the place.

For instance, I'm sitting here writing this, but I'm also thinking about what I'm going to have for lunch (soup, sandwich, or leftover lasagna?) and probably subconsciously getting scared about the talk I have to give tomorrow—and sometimes ideas will pop into my head, and then I have to dash off and write a story.

Will a machine ever think in several directions like that? And is my mind really moving freely (at will) across these different areas, or is it just reacting to stimuli (sounds, sights, smells) that I haven't consciously registered?

Can thinking and feeling be separated?

In humans I don't think they can. For example, I'll think, "There are birds outside my window eating the apples on the apple tree again." At the same time, I appreciate their colors and I laugh at how greedy they look with apple all over their beaks, and I wish they'd eat the apples on the ground instead of hogging all the best ones on the tree (I want some of those apples too …).

Do you think machines could have feelings?

I'm not sure; but if they did, might they be such different feelings that we couldn't recognize them?

Sometimes we "project" motives or emotions onto machines—we treat them as if they had human feelings or intentions. For example, when my car starts, I say, "Good car," and when it doesn't ("won't") start, I yell at it (my car always decides not to start when I'm running late). But I know that the car is behaving like a car, it isn't really being helpful or obstinate.

There are people who say that when machines reach the level of complexity of human brains, they may show the first signs of consciousness—be aware of themselves and perhaps have emotions.

Others argue that no matter how complex machine brains become, they'll only do what we program them to do—they'll never have an original idea.

But is any idea really new—or do we just take bits of data from all around us and put them together in various ways ... just as a complex machine might?

What about robots?

A robot is just a machine that's made to look a bit like a human, and programmed to look as though it has human-like reactions. It would be possible to program your computer at school to

63

groan every time you made a spelling mistake, or to whine, "I don't want to go to sleep now!" whenever you turned it off. It would sound as though it had emotions, but they'd just be imitations.

P.S. Remember that robots in movies are make-believe. K9, R2D2, and C3PO may look real, and seem to be able to think and feel—but they are really just props being manipulated by human actors.

How do humans think?

There are incredible arguments about this. Some people see our brains as sort of biological computers, others think consciousness means they are quite unlike computers. It's clear that the human mind isn't just one unit like a single computer. It's more like lots of separate units that each carry out a particular function, like using language or understanding shapes or remembering music—but these units also seem to work together and sometimes even change whatever they are doing, in ways we don't yet understand.

Do aliens exist?

Are there any aliens?
Yes.
No.
Maybe.
Probably.
This is a complicated question—you
need to digest a few more questions
and answers before my answer to this
one will make sense. The first one is
"Are there any other planets like
Earth?"

Are there any other planets like Earth?
There may be. If the Universe goes on forever, there must be an infinite number of
planets and so some of them **may** be just like
ours … (I think). Until recently, though, we didn't
even know if there were any other solar systems with
planets in the Universe, because the light from planets is too dim to see
from Earth.

Then in 1995 Michel Mayer and Didier Queloz from the Geneva Obser-
vatory studied 142 sun-like stars and finally found a star (or sun—our sun
is a star) that "wobbled" as if it were influenced by a planet. So for the first
time we had evidence of other planets in the Universe—not just stars!
Since then, at least another eight planets have been discovered—we think.
Until we actually see them, we won't know for sure.

Is there any life on those planets?
They're too far away to tell—but probably not. The one orbiting 70 Virginis is the most likely. It's about half an astronomic unit (AU) away from its sun—so it may have a temperature of about 80°C. (An AU is the distance between Earth and our sun—about 100 million miles or 150 million kilometers.) It's the only one that looks as though it might have liquid water, which is probably essential for there to be any life of the kind we know. It's just possible that there may be large molecules—very simple life—floating around in its atmosphere. But as it's got a mass at least 6.5 times that of Jupiter, any multi-celled life as we know it would be squashed flat.

There's another possibility. The planet near Virginis might have rocky moons with atmospheres and water and even life on them—but the planet moves in an elliptical orbit, coming very close to the sun and then moving a long way away, so that any life would have to cope with incredible extremes.

Where is the most likely place to find a planet like Earth?
There's a star called 18 Scorpii (number 18 in the constellation of Scorpius) that looks much more like our sun than any other star that we've studied. Our sun is a very bright G-type star—yellow stars that burn hydrogen into helium in their centers. Only 4 percent of suns are G-type stars like ours; 18 Scorpii is one of them.

How far away is 18 Scorpii?
About 46 light years from Earth. You can see it, but you'd probably need to use a telescope.

Aren't there any nearer stars that are like our sun?
Alpha Centauri is another yellow star and it's much closer—only 4.35 light years away. But it's got two companion stars. It's more likely that a single star like our sun and 18 Scorpii will have planets with stable orbits, because with two stars pulling at it, a planet might swing close to one star and be very hot, then swing way out and freeze. The climate might be too extreme for life to exist.

Colored Stars

Young, hot stars look white, cooler stars are yellow, and older stars burn red—if you look at the sun at sunset, it's red because you're looking at it through a thick, often dusty atmosphere. The stars we can most easily see are the hottest, brightest ones—the white ones. But if you train yourself to look for color differences, you will start to see that light from the stars and planets does vary—enough to say that one is "blue" and another is "red," one has a greenish glow and another is rather yellow.

I'm unique!

Could there be raccoons and humans and horses on any of the new planets?
Probably not. Life on a different planet will be … well, different. Remember that on this planet only North America has anything like raccoons and coyotes.
Even in parts of the world that have a climate like ours and soil like ours, you don't get raccoons. So even

if a planet is just like Earth, you mightn't get anything that's at all like a raccoon or a human being.

Have humans discovered any aliens yet?
Maybe—but so far the only ones we've met appear to be microscopic fossils, crystals a bit like ones produced by some Earth bacteria ... very, very simple forms of life.

These crystal "aliens" arrived on a meteorite that was collected in Antarctica in 1984. Astronomers believe that about 15 million years ago a giant meteor or comet crashed into Mars and sent this meteorite flying off into space—then onto Earth about 13,000 years ago. But there's also a good chance that these "aliens" are really from Earth—i.e., that they "invaded" the meteorite after it got here.

Spacemen see aliens ... ?
American astronauts Ed Gibson and William Pogue once saw hundreds of weird purple sparkling objects clustered around their spaceship, following them in space!
When they investigated, they found out the sparkly things were just bits of aluminum-coated plastic William Pogue had torn off during some repair work to the spaceship—but for a while they really thought they'd found UFOs (or that UFOs had found them ...).

Could there still be life on Mars?

Probably not. Most scientists believe that life needs water, and it's been billions of years since there was liquid water on Mars. It is just possible that there may be hot springs near Martian volcanoes—and there may be water there. But we'll have to wait till Mars is explored further to find out.

The scientist James Lovelock believes that anything that is alive gradually changes its surroundings to suit it. Grazing deer create more grasslands, pine trees make the soil more acidic so pine trees can flourish—and so if there is life on Mars, it should have modified Mars by now. But there are no signs that it has.

What killed Mars?

The little bit of atmosphere that is left is mostly carbon dioxide. Maybe the rest of it reacted with Martian rocks and was used up. Mars has a much more "eccentric" orbit than Earth—it swings much further away from the sun. It may be that most of Mars' atmosphere, as well as its water, is locked up in ice caps at the poles.

Could there be life on another planet in our solar system?

Probably not, if life needs water to survive. But there is a chance of it on Titan.

What is Titan?

Titan is one of Saturn's moons. There's probably quite a bit of water ice on it. But unless Saturn has volcanoes that are melting the ice, there probably isn't life there now.

In six billion years' time, when the sun turns into a red giant and expands out towards Saturn—well, maybe the ice will melt and life will evolve then.

Anywhere else?

One of Jupiter's moons, called Europa, looks as if it might be suitable for some form of life. The spaceship Galileo beamed back pictures of what look like icebergs floating on water or slushy ice. This was a surprise—scientists expected Europa would be too cold to have oceans; perhaps the constant stretching and squeezing by Jupiter's gravity makes it warmer.

But even if we find a place that is suitable, does it mean life has evolved there?

No. But now that we have realized that life can be created by a series of chemical reactions, it's likely that **somewhere** else in the Universe the right conditions occurred for life to begin.

Then where are all the aliens?

Good question. I don't know. Maybe they just can't get here. I mean, you can't exactly catch a bus to the other end of the Universe. Our nearest planet is at least 4.5 light years away.

Earth is a long way away from any other solar system—definitely in the wrong place for dropping in on neighbors. In other parts of the galaxy there are clusters where you get 100,000 stars crammed into 30 light years. This makes it much more suitable for interplanetary tourism.

But on the other hand, people are developing all sorts of ideas about how to travel immense distances through space—harnessing black holes, suspended animation. If we could reach even 20 percent of the speed of light, we'd be at the closest stars in a few decades.

Wouldn't aliens have discovered already how to travel in space?
Maybe they don't **want** to get here—or just haven't found us. Or maybe there is life out there in the rest of the Universe, but it's just a few blobs of seaweed or floating bacteria—not the sort of neighbors who build rocket ships! It didn't take long to get really simple life on Earth, but it took a heck of a long time to get anything complicated.

Early life on Earth was single-celled. That was roughly 4 billion years ago. Multi-celled life didn't evolve till 0.7 billion years ago, and intelligent life, even the simplest intelligent life, till a few million years ago. So the chance of intelligent life evolving on a planet is much, much less than the chance of just a bit of a wriggle here and there.

Do you think there's intelligent life anywhere else?
Probably—but even if there is, we may not be able to talk to it. Humans aren't even very good at communicating with dogs and cats and we've lived together on the same planet for thousands of years. When you say "sit" to your dog, he sits down, so he understands you—but do you understand him when he says "Woof"?

How do you think you can understand an alien if you can't understand a dog? What would you say to a two-headed, ocean-dwelling octopus that spoke to its friends by vibrating its tentacles against the water? Life has to be pretty much like us for you and I to understand and talk to it.

And it's taken four billion years for us to even get to the point of asking, "Are we alone in the universe?"

73

Suppose an alien ...

Suppose an alien lands in your backyard—I mean a
really **alien** alien—what would you do? What would you say?
Would you point to the house and say "house"?
(And hope that they'd point to their spaceship and go "Grrolg!")
You could just smile and hold out your hand.
(But among certain great apes smiling is seen as a threat ...)
Many scientists think we'd be able to communicate with an alien using
math. To build the rocket ships and calculate how to get to another planet,
they'd need to use math. I wonder! The ones that travel in space won't
necessarily be the math whizzes (we send astronauts, not rocket builders).
What if they don't even use language at all—they might
communicate with blinks or smells or changing colors ...
Anyway—back to the alien in your garden.

What would **you** do?

What sort of signals might aliens send us?
Maybe laser or radio signals—something regular or with a pattern
to it, so when we hear it we can say, "That can't be natural."

Are we listening for those sorts of signals?
Yes. The SETI (Search for Extra Terrestrial Intelligence) program was set up by
NASA to search for extra-terrestrial radio signals. It's no longer operating, but
there are people in universities and observatories all around the world that

are listening too, as well as the SETI League. This is a group of volunteers across the world who have replaced the government-sponsored programs.

The Australian Search for Extra Terrestrials Center is using the Parkes telescope to listen to **eight million** radio channels!

What do they listen for?

They look for radio signals that are confined to a very narrow range of frequencies. All naturally occurring radio signals span a much wider range. Even if they find signals in this band that aren't made by aliens, these might be something totally new to science—which will be a pretty big discovery anyway.

Can anyone listen for aliens?

Yes, if you have enough money to set up a radio receiver, computer and software, and satellite dish. This can cost between $1,000 and $7,000. You can then contact the SETI League in New Jersey and join the SETI program. The SETI League is on the Internet at http://seti1.setileague.org.

Have we heard anything yet?

No—nothing that's been reported anyway.

Does every intelligent society put out radio waves?
No—a few hundred years ago there wouldn't have been any radio waves from Earth, and in another hundred years we may well not use radio waves any more—we'll have come up with something better.

How can we let the Universe know that there's intelligent life on Earth?
There have been lots of suggestions. One astronomer in the 19th century suggested filling a 20-mile lake in the Sahara with kerosene and setting fire to it. Another suggested signaling in Morse code using giant mirrors.

A few years ago, a plaque and a gold-plated copper record explaining where Earth was and how to get to it were attached to the Voyager and Pioneer space-craft. These are now speeding into deep space. But it will be tens of thousands of years before they reach the nearest stars.

What happens if someone finds a sign of alien life?
If a person in the SETI League picked up an alien signal, first of all they'd make sure there was no other explanation for it. Then they'd notify the Central Bureau for Astronomical Telegrams of the International Astronomical Union, which registers all new astronomical discoveries. Then they'd contact the Secretary-General of the United Nations, then publish the findings so they were available to scientists all over the world.

And then we'd send a message back?
Probably not. Many countries—including Australia and the USA—believe that we shouldn't contact any sign of life we find on another planet.

But we sent out the Voyager record.
Opinions have changed since then. Many people feel that it's possible life on another planet might not be friendly—and that we'd need to consider the consequences carefully before we approached them.

Why might aliens be unfriendly?
Well, humans are pretty unfriendly to most species. We tend to see them either as competitors or as food or as useful in some other way. We've got where we are by being pretty ruthless to other animals—and to our human enemies. If there is another "top of the planet" species, it's possible it could be rather savage.

But wouldn't another advanced species be too intelligent to want to attack Earth?
Not necessarily. We're intelligent and have spaceships—but we are still warlike.

They might be time travelers or creatures from below the surface of the earth or from another dimension or monsters from deep in our imaginations!

Holy CROW!

Is a space war likely?

Don't worry about it. The distances are really too great to worry about a space fleet attacking us. By the time it got here, the "people" who had decided to send it would probably be dead.

What is there to worry about then?

Well, if they are much more advanced than us, we might accept their culture and their technology, lose our own and just become their "pets."

Do UFOs exist?

Of course. UFOs are just that—Unidentified Flying Objects. You can find a reasonable explanation for most UFOs—a lot of people mistake the evening star or weather balloons or shifting lights from marsh gas for a UFO.

There are some cases, however, that no one has been able to explain. But it's a big jump from seeing something strange in the sky—or even a strange craft landed in a field or beings in silver suits—to then assuming they're aliens from another planet.

The CIA confesses!

The CIA (Central Intelligence Agency) has admitted that lots of "UFO" sightings in the 1950s and 1960s were really high-altitude spy planes that it didn't want to own up to. In other words, the UFOs existed—they just weren't aliens!

Alien invasion!

Back in the 1940s, thousands of people fled from cities all over North America when a radio report declared that aliens had invaded and were spreading throughout the country. Highways were packed, people panicked … Actually it was all just a radio play based on a story by H.G. Wells about the day Martians invaded. But people believed it. We've all heard so much about aliens, even if it has been fiction, that if something strange were to happen, we might think it was aliens.

But what about people who've been kidnaped by aliens?

There has never been any **proof** that anyone has been captured by aliens.

Some of the people who claim to have been kidnaped have had something strange happen to them—but there's no proof that they met creatures from another planet. And if so many people had been kidnaped, you'd think there would be **some** proof by now.

But how can you explain all the strange things that have happened?

There are various possibilities. They might have been kidnaped by a mad hypnotist or a gang of disguised drug runners who test their new drugs on people they've kidnaped, or maybe they wandered into a cloud of hallucinogenic gas. You might say that those are all pretty unlikely; but then, so are aliens.

One of the reasons I don't think the reports of aliens visiting Earth are very likely is that the aliens seem so much like humans. I don't think that life on two different planets in separate solar systems would look so much alike.

Maybe far back in the past really advanced aliens went through the Universe genetically engineering creatures on every planet, so they were part alien—and that's why the aliens look a lot like us.
That would make a good science fiction story. In fact the idea has been used many times. But there is no reason yet to think it might have happened.

Does anything move faster than light?
Maybe. Some scientists believe that tiny forces called tachyons exist, which travel faster than the speed of light—and that maybe tiny particles called neutrinos might sometimes zap off at the same sort of speed. If they do, then "faster than light" might be possible. But don't hold your breath.

How could aliens get here?
They'd have to use a faster-than-light drive—if it were possible. But even if they did and it took them, say, two weeks to get here, to everyone they left at home it would seem to take about 500,000 years. (According to the theory of relativity, as you go faster your clocks slow down compared with those of anyone watching you.) What's the use of aliens zapping over here at almost

the speed of light when everything will be dead—or very different—when they get back home?

Think about the aliens' spacecraft too. How do they get enough power to dash across the Universe? There are no gas stations across the Universe—and they'd have to carry so much, they'd be too heavy to get here. They wouldn't be close enough to suns for solar power. Remember, they are traveling between solar systems, where suns would be as faint and distant as stars—which of course they are. Even nuclear fusion wouldn't work: the amount of fuel needed would be about 7,000 times the mass of the rocket ship.

Could aliens get our diseases? Or we get theirs?
Good point. If aliens are enough like us that they can breathe our atmosphere, then they may well be able to get sick with our diseases—and as our diseases would be new for them, they'd have no resistance. Or the aliens may be so different that they can't suffer from our diseases.

But so many people believe in aliens! Can they all be wrong?
Yes, they can. Most people used to believe the Earth was flat, that frogs came down in the rain, and that human behavior could be assessed from the shape of people's foreheads.

A hundred years ago, lots of people—often quite intelligent, educated people—saw mermaids, and before that, lots saw angels and fairies and elves. These people weren't nutcases—they just saw something odd; and because other people had said they'd seen fairies or mermaids, they thought they were seeing fairies or mermaids too, instead of looking for an alternative explanation. The same goes for stories of kidnapings by aliens and angels. If people have strange experiences, they are likely to come up with explanations for them that match their expectations.

Vampire Attack!

One dark, dark night when I was nine, I heard something scream and howl and scrape against the window as it crawled into my baby sister's room. I was convinced it was a vampire out to suck her jugular vein, but I didn't have enough courage to try to save her. Of course it was just a possum on the windowsill. I didn't know possums screamed—but I knew all about vampires. The most terrifying, blood-curdling screams a friend of mine has ever heard were out in the bush at night. She was sure it was a woman being tortured at knifepoint; it turned out to be a cat!

P.S. This is a test. Try it on your best friend.
How long do vampires live?
How long do possums live?

Most of us know more about vampires, which are imaginary, than we do about the possums that live with us in North America.

If most people believe something, doesn't that mean it's more likely to be true?
It depends what sort of thing we're talking about. If 100 people saw a dog cross the road and 99 said it was black and one said it was white, then probably the majority would be right. (But it is still interesting to find out why the one person "saw" a white dog.)

Knowledge about the way the world works is different. The knowledge that "most people" have usually lags behind the understanding that scientists have. For example, a few hundred years ago most people still believed the sun went around the Earth—even though scientists by then knew it didn't. In the 1800s, everyone "knew" that mists caused disease, but doctors knew otherwise.

The fact that "everyone" believes something may be a good reason to look at it closely and see if it is in fact true.

But why do people nowadays believe in aliens instead of in elves or fairies?
I think humans dream of aliens because at heart we're explorers. Now that all of the world has been explored, the only place to dream about is space.

83

Is time travel possible?

Is time travel possible?

A few years ago, no one could have given you a sensible answer on time travel. There were endless stories about people traveling in time, and some movies—but they didn't actually explain how it could be done. Now there is a theory about time travel, involving wormholes—not worms in the ground, but worms in the sky.

What are wormholes?

A wormhole is a tunnel through the fabric of space-time. You could fall into one somewhere past Alpha Centauri, say, and come out a few hours later near Earth. If the ends of the tunnel were moving relative to each other, you might also travel back or forth in time.

How?

Good question. To explain what wormholes and space-time are, I'd have to explain the theory of relativity and quantum theory, and to do that in two paragraphs is just about impossible. If you're really interested in wormholes, you can read some of the books listed at the back to find out more about it. But it does mean that, in theory at least, time travel is possible. And scientists are now looking at ways to find wormholes in space or make a small wormhole themselves.

85

If it is possible to travel back in time, where are all the time travelers?
Maybe they've been told to be very, very careful and not be seen. Or
maybe it's possible but uses an incredible amount of energy, so it isn't done
very often; or it can only be done under really unusual conditions—like
falling down a wormhole. There are other problems with traveling in time
too. The most famous is the "dead grandfather" problem.

What's the dead grandfather theory?
Suppose you're a time traveler and you go back to before you were born
and kill your grandfather—then you would never be born ...

   Exactly. It's a paradox—whichever way you look at it, it doesn't come out
right; which is one of the reasons time travel may be impossible. One
answer to this is to say that if you do go back and kill your grandfather,
then you create a parallel universe.

So I never go back to kill my grandfather.

So you do get born and you do go back and kill your grandfather. Hey, this isn't making any sense.

What is a parallel universe?
Imagine a building with a lot of similar but not identical rooms side by side—
and each one of those rooms is a universe. But then you're not traveling back
in time—just to a parallel universe.

Even so, we should have lots of travelers from the future of parallel universes.

If someone had invented a time machine in the future, then you'd think that lots of people would be using it—and coming back here and to lots of places in the past. But there **aren't** millions of people from the future popping up all over the place—not even from parallel futures.

So it looks as though time travel isn't as easy as all that.

Maybe we can only ever travel to the future.

But if we travel to the future, then we'd have to be able to come back, and that's traveling to the past. And traveling to the future might just be to a parallel future—there might still be another future somewhere where we didn't travel.

How space travelers go to the toilet!

How do you go to the toilet when there is no "down"?

Astronauts strap on a special toilet seat that fits snugly over their bottoms. There's a suction system to pull urine "down" and away. There are often "accidents," though. The stuff floats about in the spaceship ... and no one wants to own it!

Astronauts also have "waste collection" devices in their spacesuits, attached to their underwear with Velcro; and there's a valve to stop the stuff leaking back. They can wear diapers, too, both ordinary commercial ones (large size) and special super-absorbent ones.

WASTE COLLECTION

87

What killed the dinosaurs?

Dinosaurs were around for about 160 million years. Then, about 65 million years ago, about two-thirds of all life on the planet was wiped out—including almost all the dinosaurs. We now know that some dinosaurs survived to evolve into birds. Other prehistoric reptiles, such as crocodiles and turtles, that lived in the age of the dinosaurs are little changed from those times.

So what made most of the dinosaurs extinct?
There are several possible reasons and theories for dinosaur extinction.
◊ The dinosaurs (but for some reason not the turtles and frogs and birds) were killed when what is believed to be an asteroid somewhere in diameter between 100 and 200 kilometers (60 and 125 miles) crashed into what is now the Gulf of Mexico. There would have been a giant explosion, massive earthquakes all over the world, tidal waves—and I mean **big** ones—and, even worse, a sort of "permanent winter" or darkness, caused by clouds of dust and debris that would have covered the Earth for a long period of time and blocked out sunlight. After that there would have been an Ice Age. Apart from the direct effect of the cold (dinosaurs, like all reptiles, are very sensitive to changes in temperature), swamps, lakes, and seas would have dried up and plants would have stopped growing, so plant-eaters didn't have anything to eat; and as the plant-eaters became fewer, meat-eaters would have starved too.
◊ Dinosaurs died after exposure to poisons and disease.
◊ Dinosaurs died out slowly over one or two million years as the inland seas dried up.

◊ The Earth passed through the dense core of a giant molecular cloud over, say, a million years. Earth would have become much colder and there would have been a lot more comets around to hit Earth; both of these would have helped extinctions.

◊ Earth was cooled with dust as several giant comets "dumped" their dust into the solar system.

◊ The Earth's magnetic poles were reversed and there was a natural Ice Age.

All these theories suggest that it was the Earth getting much colder (some theories add explosions/tidal waves) that pushed the dinosaurs to extinction.

There's one theory that suggests the Earth got too hot.

◊ Maybe the million cubic meters of lava that gushed onto the Earth's surface at the end of the Cretaceous period (that's when the dinosaurs disappeared) pushed masses of carbon dioxide into the air, warming the Earth and causing tsunamis and acid rain.

How much is a dinosaur worth?

"Sue," the most complete tyrannosaurus skeleton ever found, sold for US$8.4 million in 1997 after a court battle over who actually owned her. If you find a dinosaur fossil in Canada, who it belongs to depends on whether you find it on government-owned land or private land.
If it is government land, it belongs to the government.
If it is your own property, it belongs to you.

Could Earth be hit by an asteroid?

Small asteroids and meteorites collide with Earth's atmosphere all the time (some of them, if they are big enough, will break through the atmosphere and actually hit the Earth), but often they are small and will burn up in the atmosphere before they actually hit the ground.

What about big asteroids?
A one-kilometer-wide (.62-mile-wide) asteroid will crash into the Earth roughly once every 100,000 years. There's about a 1 in 100 chance that a 100- to 200-meter (330- to 660-foot) asteroid will hit the Earth in any one year.

What would that do?
It could cause a tsunami 100 meters (330 feet) high, wipe out coastal cities, and change the climate dramatically—especially if it fell in the ocean, sending up clouds of steam. And of course if it fell on a seaboard city like New York or Vancouver …

Can we stop a giant asteroid hitting us?
Well, we can't get out of the way, but we might be able to change its direction or blow it up (using a nuclear bomb) before it reached us—

though some scientists think that would be even more dangerous; we could then be hit with all the scattered parts of the asteroid, which would now be radioactive as well!

How can we know when one is going to hit us?
By watching what's in the sky now and calculating the orbit of some of the bigger chunks of rock and ice, and working out if they'll ever be in the same place as Earth.

Has North America ever been hit by a tsunami?
Yes. The most recent one was in 1964, and was caused by an earthquake in Alaska. The tsunami traveled all the way from Alaska south to the twin cities of Alberni and Port Alberni, British Columbia, causing millions of dollars of damage to those cities.

How often do we get them?
They don't really come on schedule. We may not have one for hundreds of years or we may get a few in a decade.

What about volcanoes?
Have there ever been active
volcanoes in North America?
Not many on the continent of North America. In 1980, Mount St. Helen's, a volcano in the state of Washington, erupted. Before that, there hadn't been an active volcano on the mainland since 1921 in California. However, the Hawaiian Islands are an active volcano center.

Why isn't life fair?

Why SHOULD life be fair?
This isn't a cop-out. Just think about it ... Fairness is a concept we humans have made up to help us get along with each other. If your brother says, "Let's buy a watermelon and share it" and then hogs most of it, that isn't fair, because he's broken the agreement.

If your best friend says something really nasty about you to someone else, that isn't fair either, because friends implicitly agree to help and support each other. You don't have to say to your friend, "Look, I'll always say nice things about you if you say nice things about me"—it's taken for granted that that's what friendship is all about.

But there isn't an agreement between you and the Universe—you do this and I'll do that in exchange.

So there's no reason for one person having a happy life while someone else has an unhappy one?
Well, if there is a reason, it's hard to find. We all know that terrible things happen to some people and not to others. Some people do appear to "have all the luck." Life **isn't** fair—and it'll just break your heart if you expect it to be.

People say, "Luck is what you make it," and this is often true. Take a close look sometime at people you regard as "lucky"— successful people, happy people, fulfilled people. A surprising number will have had really horrible things happen to them in the past, but they refused to be cast down by them. They kept on going—and they worked.

I live in a beautiful valley with a garden full of birds and animals, fruit trees and roses. There's a creek 50 meters (165 feet) from the house, with clear, fresh water running over rocks. I get furious when people say, "It's Paradise— you're lucky!" It wasn't luck; it was something we searched for and built up over 20 years of hard work. If there's been "good luck" (in other words, unexpected good things) over that time, there's been "bad luck" too.

So to some extent I think that life is what you make it; but there is an element of luck—or Fate—that we can't do anything about. If you happen to be standing under a meteor when it crashes down, or you're a kid in a city being bombed, it's not your fault and there's nothing you can do to change it.

**What about murder and poverty and wars —
why do bad things happen in the world?**
◊ One answer to that is to say that God gave humans "free will"—the choice of being either good or bad rather than behaving like robots, who have no choice—and this means that bad things happen because of humans' bad actions. But if your best friend gets cancer, or is zapped by a tsunami or meteor, it's no one's fault.
◊ Another answer is that if bad things didn't happen, we would not appreciate the good things—to be happy we also have to know unhappiness. But happiness and unhappiness aren't equally distributed. Some people do have more bad things happen to them than others.

◊ A religious answer might be that these people need these things to happen to them, either for their own development or for some other reason in God's plan.

◊ And another response might be "Why not?"—in other words, there's no overall plan or fairness in the Universe.

Why do bad things happen to us?

Because it's good for us? Because we made wrong choices? Because God is unfair? Because the Universe isn't fair or unfair?

What do **you** think?

Why do SO MANY bad things happen in the world?

See above ... but I'll add this answer too. When something bad happens to us—a supposed best friend says something nasty about you, someone dies, or you do badly in an exam that you've worked quite hard for—it makes the whole world seem bad. Even if there are other good things around—loving people, close friends, cuddly animals, interesting things to do, beautiful places to see—you don't notice them. You're hung up on what went wrong.

Mostly this is a good thing in the long run. If something has gone wrong, you need to concentrate on it, come to terms with it—to correct it if you can or just work out "Where do I go from here?"

But even if two or three or even 83 things go wrong—don't feel the whole world is against you.

It isn't. Only little bits of it.

P.S. When bad things happen to me, I find the best way to get over them is to throw myself into **doing** something. Everyone is unhappy sometimes, but that's different from being depressed. Being depressed is when you feel powerless—as though there's nothing you can do.

But there is always **something** you can do—and the sooner you get involved in doing it, the sooner you'll feel better. Best of all is doing something with other people, if you can manage it.

What do you think about suicide?

I think that killing yourself is a tragedy—because days, weeks, or months later you might have felt better. **Everything** generally passes, good and bad, if you wait long enough.

People commit suicide because they are overcome by the bad things in life—pain or loneliness or horrible things that happen to them or the people they love. These things may be so overwhelming that they can't see any hope in the future—just like a sick person may not have the strength to get out of bed. This is why people who are unhappy or depressed need help.

Sometimes they just need help from friends or neighbors until they can get through the bad time.

Sometimes, though, they may need help from doctors or counsellors. Depression can be a form of illness and can be treated medically just as a bad case of the flu can be treated medically. If you were rock climbing and were suddenly faced with a great sheer cliff that you felt you couldn't possibly manage on your own, an experienced rock-climbing instructor would show you how to handle it.

If you know someone who is very unhappy—especially if they are too unhappy to sleep properly, or if they seem to be unhappy for no concrete reason, or if they've been unhappy for a long time, maybe weeks—then it is a good idea to ask for advice from a doctor or a counsellor—someone who has experience in this area and knows what to do. A good counsellor can show you how to find strategies to cope with and get over your problems.

What if you know things WON'T get better?—if you are dying of cancer and in terrible pain, and you know you won't get better? Okay, possibly then. But even in this case, better pain control might make you feel you want to keep living. I am very worried that if we get used to people killing themselves when they're ill and in pain, then we might start expecting people to kill themselves to save us the trouble of looking after them.

(Looking after someone who is dying is hard—but it can also bring people closer. I watched my father nurse my stepmother when she was dying of cancer—and though he suffered too, he learned more about happiness in those years than he ever had before. I'm not saying pain is good—but it doesn't have to be all bad either.)

Should someone be allowed to commit suicide if they want to?

I don't think it should be illegal; my view is that society only has the right to stop us hurting other members of society—not ourselves. But I think it's our duty as human beings to do everything possible to convince a depressed person that suicide isn't the best path. Life is short—and I don't want anyone to waste any of it.

NB: There are "suicide hotlines" in all telephone directories, where anyone in trouble can call. If you really feel down or if someone you know is really depressed—get help!! (You won't be intruding—most people get a real buzz from helping others ... come to think of it, helping others may be one of the things that makes us human too!)

How can I make the world better?

Good question. Now if you'll just sit still for the next three years, I'll try to answer it. Okay—in a nutshell (because otherwise this book would be too long):

1. Accept the fact that you can't make the world perfect—it never will be. If you can accept that, you'll be happy with what you have changed, rather than always depressed at how much there is to be done.
2. Now find a cause to work for that you feel passionate about, or maybe two or three causes—but not so many that you never have time to do much for any of them.

3. Next—work out the most effective way to make change happen. Sometimes having a rally or sit-in can be a good way to convince people to think as you do—or to stand up and say they do. But sometimes it can have the opposite effect, and make people think, "Oh, they're just ridiculous—what they're saying must be rubbish." Decide what will work, and what won't.

(I once knew a girl who decided that she wouldn't eat chocolate until the Vietnam War of the 1960s and 1970s was over. It made her feel good— every time she saw a bit of chocolate, she congratulated herself on how much she was suffering. But it didn't end the war any faster.)

How would you solve the world's problems?
What causes do you feel most deeply about?
What do you think are the world's worst problems?
What do you think would be effective ways of stopping the problem?
What would be some stupid ways?

What do **you** think?

Are some people better than others?

Well, the easy answer to this question is "Yes." Lots of people see better than I do, for example (I wear glasses for reading). Lots of people sing better than I do. But if you mean "Are some people more worthy or valuable than others?" the answer is more complex. (I'd say "No," some other people might say "Yes.")

Throughout human history, people have thought others were worse—uglier or more stupid or more cunning—than they were. Sometimes they were suspicious of anyone who didn't live in their village or came from another country, or anyone who had a different religion or a different color of skin. As you go through life, you'll meet many people who'd like to believe that this or that type of person is stupid or criminal or dirty. It makes them feel better about themselves. Maybe you know someone who thinks that anyone with close-set eyes is untrustworthy, that all women are bitchy, or that men who wear suits must be boring.

If anyone makes a statement or claim about another group of people, ask:
◊ Why are they saying it?
◊ What claims do they have to support it?
◊ And if you find that you agree with them, does it matter?

Animals with glasses are very clever.

So can't you make any comparisons between groups?
Yes, but you can't apply them to individual members of the groups, because even if one race or group of people is more intelligent or less intelligent than another, the group is so big that the next person you meet of that race may be just as dumb (or as brilliant) as you are.

But you can see that some people are less clever or less talented than others?
That's true, but beware of being too judgmental or scornful about them. We all have faults—my study is always a mess, and I can't spell (I'm dyslexic), and my handwriting is almost impossible to read. Yet I am good at other things (and I've published 60 books!).

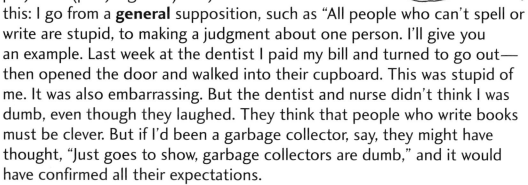

We also have to be careful not to show prejudice (pre-judgment). Prejudice works like this: I go from a **general** supposition, such as "All people who can't spell or write are stupid, to making a judgment about one person. I'll give you an example. Last week at the dentist I paid my bill and turned to go out—then opened the door and walked into their cupboard. This was stupid of me. It was also embarrassing. But the dentist and nurse didn't think I was dumb, even though they laughed. They think that people who write books must be clever. But if I'd been a garbage collector, say, they might have thought, "Just goes to show, garbage collectors are dumb," and it would have confirmed all their expectations.

Judging any one writer or anyone, for that matter, with little reliable information to go on is bound to lead to false conclusions. And judging a **whole group** of people from one incident involving one member of the group is stupid and possibly dangerous. Prejudice is not checking whether something is true or not. Or if it is true, thinking it's more important than it is. It's easy to check facts. It's not quite as easy to be sure that the way you think makes sense.

Lower taxes for redheads?

If you knew for sure that a certain group of people caused more accidents, committed more crimes, or had a lower intelligence than you and your friends and relatives, do you think they should have to pay higher taxes, or have special laws made that apply only to them?

What if you found that a certain group of people— say, everyone with red hair—had fewer accidents, committed fewer crimes, and had a higher intelligence? Should they pay lower taxes than you do? (Often people are very willing to point out who is worse than they are, but aren't so eager to find groups that are better ...)

It is likely that the majority of crimes are committed by men. Should men therefore pay more taxes than women? Should women have better educational opportunities because they are less likely to be criminals?

What do **you** think?

Since Raccoons help society by eating most of the garbage, we should pay less taxes!

But animals don't even pay taxes at all!

Is it wrong to kill people?

What do you think? This is one of the really tricky ones. I can't say, "Yes, it's always wrong to kill people," but I don't really feel comfortable saying, "Oh, yes, sure, it's fine to kill people sometimes—just make sure you don't kill **me**."

Killing people is a social problem and a moral problem. A social problem has bad consequences for you and other people. A moral problem is caused by someone doing something wrong.

Let's look at the social problem. Human societies are based on trust. We trust that our next-door neighbor isn't going to blast us with a machine gun no matter how loudly we play rock music at 2 a.m. If we could no longer trust that the next person to come round the corner wasn't going to murder us, then we'd be too scared to go to school or work.

And if everyone were too scared to go about the things they normally do every day, society would break down. (Who'd deliver the mail or the daily papers, for starters?!)

If all of us (instead of just a rotten few) decided to kill each other, well, our lives would be short and unpleasant.

Okay. But is it WRONG to kill people? Or just a lousy idea?
All religions say it's wrong to kill people most of the time—but many say it's okay to kill your enemies, and in **some** cases you can even kill friends or relatives—old people who can no longer chew their food, babies if the

107

people already here are starving, people who are suffering and want to die. Other religions say that killing anyone is wrong, no matter what the reason.

Do you think it's ever okay to kill someone?

I think so. (I just hope I never have to do it.) The law says that if someone is trying to kill me, I can stop them with any force necessary. If I could stop them without killing them, I would. But if I couldn't, and it was the only way to save my life (or my son's life, my husband's life, my friend's life), I'd kill. And if I had enough courage, I'd kill someone to save the life of a stranger if I happened to be passing by—when I was sure that I knew who was attacking whom.

But if there was any way at all I could stop them without killing them, I'd do that—and I'd choose the way that hurt them least, too.

When is it o.k. to kill someone?

Would you kill someone?

Imagine a guy with a knife is about to stab you. You grab the knife
and just as he's about to strangle you, you …? What do you do?
Or you're in the army and your government says, "Fight the enemy.
Fight to kill." What do you do?

What if you don't think they're an enemy at all? (A lot of people had to
make this decision in the 1960s when the Vietnam War was going on.
People who didn't think the Vietnamese were enemies were still chosen by
ballot to go into the army.) Should you be able to make
your own decision about what to do?
What would happen if everyone in our army made their own decision
every time they were asked to fight? Wouldn't the army fall to pieces?
(You might think this would be a good thing—if every army did this,
we mightn't have wars. But what if another country attacked us
and their army fought no matter what?)

What do **you** think?

Are there any other times you might kill someone?
If someone were in desperate agony and wanted me to kill them so they
could escape the pain … well, I think I'd try to find any possible way to
stop their pain first, because if I could do that, they might not want to die.
(And I'd hate to live in a world where, when pain or trouble got too bad,
people were expected to kill themselves.) Death can seem an easy way

out—it means you don't have to feel guilty that people are lonely or in pain when you haven't done enough to help them.

What about people who kill but not in self-defense? Will a murderer always be a danger to other people?
No. Often they are just mentally ill and need looking after. We wouldn't kill someone who was so sick they needed constant looking after—so maybe we shouldn't kill someone who is so mentally ill they need guarding all the time to stop them raping or killing others.

Are there any really evil people?
I don't know. I just don't know. Is it always an evil nature that makes a person want to hurt someone else? Or do people lash out because they've been hurt themselves in the past and were brought up with people who lived angry, brutal lives, so they don't know any other way to react? Or because they are mentally ill, or their hormones are out of kilter?

Could people like Hitler and Pol Pot ever have thought they were doing the right thing?
At first glance it seems silly even to ask that question—Hitler was responsible for millions of deaths in World War II and Pol Pot caused millions of deaths in Cambodia in the 1970s. What they did was undoubtedly wrong, but could they have thought they were right?

Well, it's possible. I was once hurt when a man flung me to the ground because he thought I was being attacked by a killer tomato. (Okay, you can giggle, but it wasn't funny then.) That man was mentally ill. He really did think he was saving my life, even though he was quite wrong.

So is it just possible that Hitler and Pol Pot may have thought they were right? Maybe they were mentally unbalanced. (They probably were.) Maybe they just didn't know how to really think things through, how to examine what they believed and say, "Do I have enough evidence to believe this? Am I prejudiced?"

Every day, people think they have made the right decision when they haven't. But generally these decisions don't have the tragic consequences that Hitler's and Pol Pot's did. Remember, though, it wasn't just Hitler and Pol Pot who made the bad decisions. It was also all the people who followed them, and all the people who knew they were wrong and did nothing about it.

What about war?

In a war, opposing groups agree that it's okay to kill people—as long as they're the enemy. War is not an intelligent way to solve problems— too many people get hurt (as well as squirrels, trees, baby ducks, and creatures who have no say at all in what happens).

On the other hand, if your country is already at war, what should you do?

Evacuate? Easy for them to say!

What would you do?

I hope I never have to decide. But if I did, I'd look at the war and try to decide if it's just or unjust—and if it's unjust, I'd start speaking out. I'd also try to work out what would happen if we just stopped fighting and forgot all about it—would the other side stop too? Or kill us? Is there some other way of ending the conflict?

It's a good idea to look closely at any war and see who is really pushing for it, and why. Is the cause really right? Or do certain people stand to make a lot of money or look good or gain political power?

I remember a man who worked in the arms industry saying in despair a few years ago, "Peace is breaking out all over the place." He was serious! But he cheered up a few weeks later when the war in Bosnia-Herzegovina started. Many people make a lot of money from war. (The two most profitable businesses in the world are weapons manufacture and the illegal drug trade.)

And American presidents and British prime ministers have become a lot more popular, and, so, more likely to be re-elected, when

they have arranged or engaged in a successful little war—a war that is quick, involves relatively few casualties for their troops, and has the desired outcome.

What about if there was a war overseas and one group of people was killing another? Would you kill them to stop more bloodshed?
I don't know the answer to that. If I were sure that I could stop the fighting (and if I had the courage to become involved), I might. But often killing just leads to more killing—and it can be very hard to make the right decision.

Will there always be wars?
Yes. People will always fight—over who'll have the last chocolate cookie or the mineral/oil rights in the Falkland Islands, Kuwait, or Iraq. There's a prediction that the next major war will be about water supplies.

But wars needn't be as disastrous as they are now. If we cared enough, we'd force our governments not to allow certain kinds of arms to be made or sold—nuclear weapons that leave radioactive residues lasting thousands of years, or toxic or poisonous gases, or landmines that kill and maim civilians (although in 1998 many countries signed the Ottawa Treaty, banning the use of landmines).

How do we know what is right or wrong?

There are two reasons why something might be right or wrong, good or bad. The first is a practical reason—it works better or worse that way. It is **wrong** to punch your sister, because she might punch you back. It is **right** to give poor people money or food, because otherwise they might be forced to steal or they may be malnourished.

The second is a moral or ethical reason: believing that some things are intrinsically (by their very nature) right or wrong. It is wrong to punch your sister, because that would hurt her. It is right to help others, because they need it.

There have been thousands of human societies—and while some of their rules of what's right and wrong have differed, some seem to be universal.
◊ Most societies agree that you should not kill people except under certain conditions—if they are an enemy of the country, for example, or if they have broken a major law, such as murdering a policeman. However, even when the law of the country says that murderers should be killed, there may be people within that society who disagree. Many people do not support the death penalty, and "pacifists" believe that war is always a bad solution and that another one can and should be found. But there has never been a society where there were no rules at all about killing.
◊ Most societies agree that children should be looked after, even if they don't do it very well. (Some societies have even allowed people to kill young babies.)
◊ Most societies have also agreed that the people who live in their society should obey its rules—even if they don't agree with them. All societies protect their members too, in various ways. If we pay taxes to look after

people who are sick, for instance, then we'll be looked after when we're sick.

That is really what living in a society is all about—banding together so that you can fight off the saber-toothed tigers. Or working out a way that all kids can get an education, even if they aren't rich.

I support banding together to fight off all the saber-toothed tigers.

Does everyone have a moral code—principles that they live by?
Yes. Most people haven't **worked out** what rules they live by—they do things on automatic pilot. But everyone at some time thinks, "It's right to do this" or "It's wrong to do that." And whenever they think that, they are living by their moral code. In fact, there are moral judgments going on all around us. Every book or movie has a moral message. Even adventure movies make all sorts of statements about what's right and wrong—you just don't notice they're doing it.

◊ When the hero stops the villains from cheating a million people, the movie is saying that cheating people is wrong.

◊ When the hero saves his girlfriend, the movie is saying it's your duty to save the people you love.

◊ When the hero is allowed to inflict any form of punishment, including death, on others who are robbers or traitors or mad scientists, the message is that these people can be thought of as not fully human—so the rule about not killing people doesn't apply to them.

◊ When the hero shoots at the villain in a crowded street, the movie is saying that it doesn't matter who gets in the way, or who gets hurt or killed, as long as you get what you're going after. That's what a lot of movies are saying nowadays—you see the hero blow up buildings or cars or firing in crowded streets, and it doesn't matter who gets hurt as long as it's not one of the main characters.

Next time you see a movie, just think about what it's **really** saying—you may find it's saying a lot of stuff you didn't notice and may not agree with once you start to think about it.

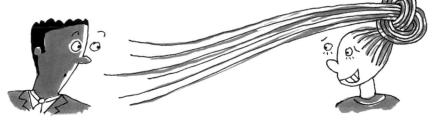

Do you ever lie?
Yes. I lie when my best friend says, "Do you like my hair?" and I say, "It looks lovely" even though it looks like … well, I won't tell you what it looks like. (But I might say, "It looks really … er, interesting," rather than actually lie about it.)

I lied when my son asked me, "Can I have a horse next birthday?" and I said, "I'll think about it." I really meant, "No, but by then I think you'll have forgotten about it."

I might lie about bigger things too, if I were afraid of what would happen if I told the truth. If soldiers were hunting for someone I'd hidden, I'd lie to keep the person safe. But I don't think I'd lie just to make things easier for myself, or to make myself seem better than I am.

Lying is okay when ... ?

Is lying okay if it doesn't do anyone else
any harm? (Do you know when something is going to do harm or not?)
Is lying a good thing if it makes someone else feel better (as when I
tell my friend her hair looks nice, or when you say you can't go to a
party because there's something else you have to do, but really
it's because you don't like the person giving it)? Or would it be
better to be friendly and polite but honest?

Perhaps lying is okay if you just do it for other people? (But then,
if everyone lies a lot, will you ever know quite what to believe?)

What are some of the situations in which you've said one thing
and meant another? Do you think you behaved well?

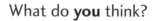

What do **you** think?

What about religious rules?
If you believe in a religious rule, you believe it's true no matter
what society you are in.

Do all religions believe the same things are good and bad?
No. But there's amazingly widespread agreement about the big items—the
sacredness of life, the necessity of caring for the frail and sick, and honoring

the Creator, previous generations, your elders. The differences tend to be in areas such as diet, religious rituals and festivals, how much God/the gods will intervene in your life, whom you can marry and why.

Do all religions have rules?
Yes they do, and many religious rules make excellent sense as ways to organize a workable society.

Like what?
Like Moses' Ten Commandments in the Bible. They're the basis of the Jewish, Christian, and Muslim faiths—and if you look at them closely, only one of them mentions God. The others are ways to keep society functioning smoothly.

You can read them yourself—but I'll summarize what they say. First, honor God and don't make any image of anything else and worship it—that's the God one; the others tell you to keep the seventh day of the week holy and don't do any work or make anyone else work for you on that day, to honor your parents, and not kill, steal, lie, commit adultery, or be jealous of other people's possessions.

(There are a lot of other commandments in Deuteronomy, the fifth book of the Bible. They tell you to give what you can to those in need and not to cut down useful trees in a siege in case you need them later; it says that a man shouldn't go away to war or on business for the first year after he's married but stay at home with his wife; and that you should always put a balustrade around the roof so that no one can fall from it. These were useful laws for a tribe that was learning to live in farms and cities.)

What about some of the other religions?
Well, according to the Dalai Lama, the essence of Buddhism is to help others if you can; if you can't, at least do no harm.

The Hopi in North America believe that the Earth is a living, growing person, and that all things on it are her children.

Then why isn't the world a better place?
Maybe because people say they believe those things, but they practice other things—like it's okay to hurt people as long as you get something out of it, that anything is okay as long as someone makes money from it, that you can do anything as long as you get away with it …

What if everyone felt like that?
Then I'd build a spaceship and go to another universe, fast. Luckily, not everyone is like that. But a lot of people can't see that their behavior has an effect on everyone else, because they don't think about what they do, they just copy everyone else.

P.S. Your left sock is under the sofa … and I ate the last chocolate cookie!

Some pages of impossible questions!

How do you explain red to a blind person?
My grandfather asked me this one when I was six, and I've been trying to answer it on and off ever since. (The more you think about it, the harder it gets.) If anyone has a decent answer, let me know!

What is a game?
This is one of the **great** questions of all time. (My grandfather asked me this when I was ten—I found out later he'd pinched it from a philosopher called Wittgenstein.) Do you think it sounds easy? Try it—I mean, we all know what games are, don't we?
Games are things we play.
So playing the piano is a game?
A game is something done just for fun.
Then a bubble bath is a game?
A game is a sport.
Then Monopoly isn't a game?
Or Scrabble?

If you can come up with a definition of "game" that works—I mean one that includes all the games we **know** are games and **doesn't** include any other stuff—I'll send you a copy of my next book!

What happens when Superman goes to the toilet?
Just think about this—everything is at superhuman strength, isn't it? What happens when he sneezes? No one—not even Superman—can control the strength of a sneeze. Why don't buildings blow away every time he has a cold?

Whom would you rescue?
If you saw a burning building, whom would you rescue first? Your aunt? Your best friend? Your dog? Someone's baby? An old person?

Who or what is a person?

Can an alien be a person if it looks like us and behaves like us but can't have children with a human?
If you'd been around 40,000 years ago, would you have thought the Neanderthals next door were people too?
If we find out whales are as intelligent as us, can they be people?
Are great apes people? They are at least as intelligent as a six-year-old child, and have feelings and are sort of cousins of ours anyway ...
What about computerized robots that are even more intelligent than us but don't have feelings—or a robot that's been programmed to have feelings? What about someone with severe brain damage who can't think much but who feels just as we do?
Or a sociopath (criminal) who is very intelligent but doesn't understand right and wrong the way most of us do?

What do **you** think?

How SF movies got it wrong!

There are lots of things in films, especially science fiction films,
that don't quite add up when you think about it.

In *Star Wars*, how did you hear all that stuff happening in the space
battle?—I mean, you need air or something to transmit sound.

Or in *Independence Day*, how come the giant spaceship didn't affect Earth's
tides (the moon does—and it's not nearly as close) and cause
massive tidal waves? And why didn't the energy from the existing ship
affect Earth too? For that matter, even the energy as the ship braked
should have fried all life on Earth into overcooked chips.

Asking questions about movies doesn't make them
less fun—but it really sharpens your mind, so you
stop taking other stupid stuff for granted.

Where to ask questions

Some people **hate** answering questions—especially if they don't know the answer.

Other people **love** answering questions, because it means that the person who asks is interested in the same things that they are.

If your parents, teachers, best friends just groan when you ask yet **another** question ...

◊ Ask a good librarian—who probably won't answer the question for you but will show you where to find the books, films, or Web sites that might help.

◊ Ask a minister of religion—because searching for answers to big questions is what ministers have dedicated their lives to.

◊ Write to the professor of whatever subject you are interested in at your local university. I wrote to a professor of physics when I was about your age. I wanted to know what the difference was between a living and a non-living object. He handed it on to the professor of philosophy, who sent me a list of useful books. And later on, I chose to study philosophy at university (but I still don't know the answer).

◊ Look for *New Scientist* magazine in your library or newsstand. You'll probably find a lot of it boring or hard to understand—but in each issue there'll be bits that are fascinating. It will tell you what new things are being discovered about life, death, the universe, aliens, and ethics—and it's read and written by people who keep asking questions and trying to answer them.

National Geographic and *Canadian Geographic* are worth looking at too.
◊ Look for Internet sites. NASA has one that would be good for space science; and there are many, many others that might help you answer other questions.

P.S. If you are really interested in a question, it's worth asking as many people as possible, because they'll probably all give you different answers. There may be lots of ways of looking at that question.

The bigger the question, the more answers there'll probably be.

Other books to read

Heather Couper and Nigel Henbest, *Black Holes: A Journey to the Heart of a Black Hole*, DK Publishing, 1996

Heather Couper and Nigel Henbest, *How the Universe Works: 100 Ways Parents and Kids Can Share the Secrets of the Universe*, Reader's Digest, 1994

Tim Flannery, *The Future Eaters*, Random House, 1995

Jostein Gaarder, *Sophie's World*, Berkeley Publishing Group, 1997

Anything by Stephen Jay Gould—especially the books that are collections of essays or articles

Tim Haines, *Walking with Dinosaurs: A Natural History*, DK Publishing, 2000

Louis Phillips, *Ask Me Anything About Dinosaurs*, Illustrated by Kevin Wasden, Avon Camelot, 1997

C. Claiborne Ray, *The New York Times Book of Science Questions and Answers: 200 of the Best, Most Intriguing and Just Plain Bizarre Inquiries into Everyday Scientific Mysteries*, Illustrated by Victoria Roberts, Anchor Books/Doubleday, 1997

Jeremy Weate, *Young Person's Guide to Philosophy*, Illustrations by Peter Lawman, DK Publishing, 1998

Index